To Mary,

See The World
Through My Eyes
—— *A Retrospective* ——

John J. Mora

Thanks For Being, A Positive
Role Model For Our Children!

[signature]

2-24-06

Through My Eyes — A Retrospective

Copyright © 2003 by John J. Mora

Inquiries should be addressed to:
info@thewoodmanpress.com

First Printing 2003

Cataloging-in-Publication Data
Mora, John
Through My Eyes — A Retrospective

1. Author. II. Title of Book
ISBN 0974324302

Library of Congress Control Number:
2003109310

Book and Cover design by Trey Colvin

Printed in the United States of America
at Morgan Printing in Austin, Texas

Dedicated to:

My Heavenly Father through whom all things are possible.

My loving Wife, Rode, whose constant love, support and encouragement have never failed me.

My three wonderful children, Johnny, Sophie, and Benny who continue to amaze me more and more every day.

Mom and Dad, Pablo and Tomasita Mora, who continue to be a source of inspiration in my life.

My brothers and sisters who I've always admired,

P.J. and his wife Toni Mora

Noemi Mora

Betty and her husband Ernie Ambriz

Nita Mora

Mark and his wife Lupita Mora

Manny and his wife Estella Mora

Eli Mora

All my nieces and nephews.

All of my Aunts, Uncles, and Cousins.

A special dedication to my Tia Dora.

And in loving memory of,

Tia Lile,

Grandma and Grandpa Manuel and Rosalia Z. Mora.

Abuelito and Abuelita, Emiliano and Guadalupe Guajardo

Table of Contents

Cover Photo
Circa 1968 Author with Brothers and Sisters.
From front to back: PJ, Mimi, Betty, Nita, Mark,
Manny, Eli, and John Mora (Author)

Introduction

2-26-'02

I grew up in a small south Texas town called Donna in a region of Texas known as the Rio Grande Valley. I am the youngest of my parent's eight children. My parents, Pablo and Tomasita Mora, were, and are still today, one of the biggest inspirations in my life. My siblings consist of Pablo Jr. (P.J.), Noemi (Mimi), Veronica (Betty), Nita (Weecho), Mark (Mark), Manuel (Manny), Eladio (too many nicknames to mention, but the one that has stuck the longest is "Eli"), and then there is me, Juan (John, Johnny, or Jay), the last one on the totem pole. My brothers and sisters all had a hand in my upbringing, and are still very influential in my life. My parents still live in the same house I grew up in, and even though I have not lived there for quite some time now, it's a place I still call home today, and probably always will.

I grew up during a time when it was okay for kids to play outside without having to have too much adult supervision. It was a time when neighbors took the time to get to know each other and when kids respected their elders. It was nights on end of freeze tag or kick the can. We played Cowboys and Indians, cops and robbers. We played Red Rover and Simon Says. Life was simple then.

3

Originally, I started writing these stories as a sort of history so my children could read when they were older and understand more of what it was like when I was their age. In doing so, they could also understand more of where I came from, and I could explain what I was thinking or why I did some of the things I did. I had no intention of ever getting these stories published into a book. However, here they are. These are stories of things that actually happened in my life, or as close to them as I can recall. I hope that you have as much fun reading them as I did writing them.

My Heroes, The Lone Ranger and His Trusty Sidekick

9-07-'98

Growing up in my father's house, I had many heroes. There were TV comic heroes like Batman and Robin, Superman, Spiderman, and Captain America. I had sports heroes such as Roger Staubach, Tony Dorsett, Drew Pearson, Julius "Dr. J" Ervin, Nolan Ryan and Steve Garvey. I also had local sports heroes from our hometown football team. After we would come home from a Friday night football game, I would pretend to run like Keith Frase or Kim Jackson, and I pretended to throw passes like Mitch Kityama.

Western movie good guys were always some of my favorites though. John Wayne personified one of the greatest western heroes, and I always thought of him as the true cowboy. Clint Eastwood personified the smooth quick-drawing vindicating cowboy whom you knew somehow was going to get through unscathed in the end. Then there was Dad's favorite, the Lone Ranger and his trusty sidekick Tonto. No one could rescue a damsel in distress quite as well as them. They would always escape what seemed to be sure death with miraculous feats.

Dad loved the Lone Ranger so much as a child that his friends and family nicknamed him "Loney" after the Lone Ranger. That nickname has stuck with him all his life. Still today my aunts, uncles, and cousins on his side of the family call him Tio (Spanish for Uncle) Loney. He and my aunts have told me countless stories of how every time they played, Dad had to be the Lone Ranger. He and his friend, Benito Garcia, would make their own toys out of wood, including his pistols he used as the Lone Ranger. Sometimes you can see Dad's face light up as he recounts his yesteryears as a young boy and as the Lone Ranger. I can tell he still gets excited about being the Lone Ranger.

When I was growing up, my parents were not something out of the ordinary. They loved each of their eight children the same. They spanked us when we got out of line. They consoled us when we were hurt. They provided for our needs and wants the best way they could, and we were never short on love.

Mom was, and is still today, a wonderful wife and mother. Like most moms, she always gave of herself unselfishly so that we could have some of the things we otherwise probably could not. When I was growing up, and still today, it seemed as if Mom always knew what I was thinking or feeling. Mom, like most moms, wore many hats. She was doctor, chef, psychiatrist, teacher, police, and referee. But the hat that fit her best was that of the family glue. She was the one who kept us together when the ship that we seemed to be on was falling apart. She would patch our bumps and scrapes and mend our broken hearts. She was a confidence builder when we felt down. She always seemed to make my problems disappear. If something was wrong, all I needed was a hug from her and I knew it was all going to be okay. Mom has always had a knack for making things better and her love has no end.

Dad was the protector and provider for our family. He was our leader. Dad, as is the case with most dads, was the disciplinarian. He tried to keep us in line, and we usually did not veer too far off that line. But still, Dad was, and is still today, all heart. And like Mom, Dad gave of himself unselfishly so that we could attain and have the things that we normally would not be able to. Dad also wore many hats. He was our bank, our accountant, our chauffeur, our barbe-cue king, our advisor, and our teacher. Actually, he was more like the principal. But the hat that fit him best was that of the family foundation. He was the rock we all leaned on. He supported the entire load of a family of eight children and a loving wife on his broad shoulders. And let me tell you, it was quite a load. At times the founda-tion cracked, but somehow, some way, Dad always seemed to patch himself up and not let us fall. For years he weathered the storms that included bankruptcy, not only once, but twice, feeding and clothing eight children, and giving each one of us an opportunity at higher educa-tion so that we would have a better life than that of his and Mom's. That was one thing he made sure of.

As heroes have come and gone in my life, only two have remained constant. They form a more dynamic duo than that of the caped crusaders Batman and Robin. Although mere words could never say what I truly feel for my parents, and for what they have always been and done for me in my life, I know my life is better off because of them. Dad and Mom are two of life's most ordinary people with extraordinary talents. They molded us and shaped us and helped us all become what we are today. Alone, they have the ability to shine like the brightest of stars in the night, but together they shine brighter than the sun itself. And as I look back at all those heroes I admired while I was growing up, they all seem to fail by comparison to my true heroes — Dad and Mom. Or better yet, should I say, "The Loney Ranger and his Trusty Sidekick."

I love you, Mom and Dad.

The Railroad Tracks

When I was growing up and going to high school, one of my favorite aunts, Tia Lile (pronounced Lee-leh or Aunt Lilly in English) used to pick up my brother Eli and me and take us home. She was not known for her flowery speech, but she had a heart of gold and it was as big as Texas. Since my mother could not drive, Tia Lile would give us a ride home from school every day. And although she had two sons of her own, she treated us as if we were hers as well.

My cousins, her sons, Johnny, who is the oldest, and Martin, are like brothers to me. Johnny and my brother Eli are about the same age, and Martin and I are about the same age. I always had this tremendous respect for Johnny, in whom Tia Lile instilled a warm heart, coupled with a determination to exceed and beat the odds by working hard at everything he did. I respected Martin as well, but he was more like me, a little spoiled being he was the baby of the family.

Dad usually laid down the law, but Tia Lile made sure we stayed within the law. Although she was very kind-hearted, she had a short fuse. I can remember her losing her temper and out came the expletives. I remember one of the first times I heard her go off on someone. It was during a Donna Little League baseball game between the Braves – the team me and my older brothers Manny and Eli played for – and the Colts - the team my cousin Johnny played for. Our coach objected to Johnny pitching past the third inning because he had pitched the previous game. In Little League, there's a rule which doesn't allow a pitcher to pitch more than a certain amount of innings on consecutive days, or a given time period. Johnny had already met his allotment. Tia Lile thought our coach was objecting Johnny's age. She argued with the umpire and our coach to let her son play. When the umpire ruled in favor of our coach, it infuriated her. She stormed on the field with Johnny's birth certificate and proceeded to unleash her fury on the umpire. I remember not knowing what the heck was going on at the time, but I do remember thinking, "Oh my God, Tia Lile is going to kill him." I knew then, I didn't want to be the one who made her mad.

Tia Lile was a grand lady, and although she would be the last to admit it, she had a soft side to her. I remember telling her once just how much I liked popsicles. Shortly afterwards, she brought a box of popsicles to my house and gave them to me. I was so excited; I ate the whole box that same day. She was always doing things like that for me.

One of my fondest memories of her took place one day after school. She was there to pick us up like clockwork as she always had. I cannot remember why Johnny wasn't at school that day, so it was just Martin, Eli and me. It was a warm sunny day, as most of those days in south Texas are. After all our goodbyes to all our friends and idle chit-chat we headed out of the school parking lot. Tia Lile's car had air conditioning but for some reason it was not working that day. On the way home we had to cross over some railroad tracks that were close to a very busy intersection. There was only enough room for one car between the traffic signal and the tracks. Well, maybe two, if the first car scooted up a bit. As we approached the busy intersection, the light turned red. The two cars in front of us squeezed in just beyond the tracks. I turned to my right and noticed a train coming down the tracks. I thought to myself, "Surely Tia Lile is not going to even attempt to get close to the tracks; or, needless to say, even try to cross the tracks with that train coming." To the surprise of us all, she pulled up and stopped right in the middle of the tracks with the train coming right at my door. I thought to myself, "What was she thinking! She has a car full of kids! Did she not see the train?" Actually, she had. She just did not expect it to be as close as it was. Not wanting to panic, I kept a close eye on the train and the light. I thought, as soon as the light turns green I am going to yell, "Go! Go! Go!" All of us were stunned. None of us dared speak and ruin her concentration. The train hit its loud whistle as it got closer. Surely she had a plan. I looked at her, I looked at the train, and then looked back and, darn, the light was still red. The silence in the car was deafening. Martin, Eli and

I were all pale with fear. I thought to myself, "This is it! My life is over." The train got louder and closer. We were all sweating except for Tia Lile. She looked so cool. She never let go of the steering wheel and she had one foot on the brake and the other on the gas pedal, ever so ready for the light to turn green and the cars to move out of the way. I turned and looked again and the light was still red. I turned and saw the train. It seemed like I could reach out and touch it when all of a sudden it happened. Tia Lile went ballistic. She broke the silence in the car with a slew of profanity and hand gestures that would make any rebellious teenager proud as she leaned on the horn with all her might. All of her rage and wrath was unleashed at the light, the train, and most of all those idiots in front of us that wouldn't move. Finally, the light turned green. The cars could not move out of our way fast enough as Tia Lile lowered the boom on the gas pedal. Somehow, she managed to squeeze by them and make a dash across the tracks. The train seemed to miss us by inches. She passed them on the on coming traffic side of the road, turning left at the intersection with her left hand and waving obscene gestures with the right, all the while yelling more profanities at these idiots who almost made the train crash into us for not moving. After all was said and done, we continued on down the road and no one mentioned that incident the rest of the way home. Actually, I don't remember anyone saying *anything* the rest of the way home.

Tia Lile was a lot like her mother, my grandmother, Rosa. They were tough ladies who made sure we didn't get too far out of line. However, behind all that yelling and tough nature, they were as warm as your favorite quilt on a cold winter night. Tia Lile loved me, and I have no doubt about that, but just because she loved me didn't mean she was going to let me get away with something that I was not supposed to be doing. Amidst any kind of chaos though, Tia Lile knew how to make me laugh and I will always remember her for that. There are so many more fond memories that I have of my wonderful Tia Lile and also of our daily treks home. However, none make my heart race, while bringing a tear to my eyes and a smile to my face, as much as that day on the railroad tracks.

Our Guardian Angel

──────── *11-13-'97* ────────

We have all heard of guardian angels. How
they protect us from evil and harm. How they
always seem to be there in times of trouble.
Assigned to you and you alone, specifically by
God himself. Some people claim to have more
than one. Some people claim to have seen theirs
in a flash of bright light or a smoked-filled
room, and still, some people claim they have
never seen theirs, but nonetheless believe
they have one.

My Aunt Dora (or Tia Dora as I have known
her all of my life) was, and is to this day, a simple woman. She has never prided herself in the
extravagance of life. That is not to say she does-
n't enjoy the finer things in life; it's just that she
would rather care for a person in need and give
of herself unselfishly with no questions asked.
She would rather go without so that you can
have what you need. She is definitely the kind-
est, most giving person I have ever had the
pleasure of knowing.

My grandfather became bedridden for more
than twenty years after a pair of massive
strokes, and my grandmother developed a bad
case of gangrene after stepping on a rusty nail in
her flowerbed. Grandma had one of her legs
amputated and was relegated to a wheelchair for
many years before she passed away. Tia Dora

forsook ever having a family of her own to care for her parents. She gave up dating and devoted herself to the care and needs of my grandparents. Ever vigilant by their sides, Tia Dora labored every day to make sure there was nothing they needed. She would bathe and change my grandparents. She also helped my grandmother with her grooming and makeup. She was constantly cooking and cleaning because my grandmother didn't like a dirty house.

One of the things I remember most about visiting my grandparent's house was that Tia Dora always had Oreo cookies in the cupboard. Knowing that I loved coffee, she would serve me a cup with my Oreo cookies. To this day, I still love coffee and Oreo cookies. All the grownups in my family, including my parents, smoked at the time. One of the biggest thrills we got was when they would let us take a lit cigarette butt and go throw it in the toilet. Tia Dora, though, would always leave a couple puffs on her cigarettes for us. We would run to the bathroom, take a couple of puffs, throw the butt in the toilet, and then flush. Sometimes when our parents weren't looking, she would let us light her cigarette. Even though it was a thrill for me at the time, I realized that smoking left a terrible taste in my mouth and I began to hate it. I think she was hoping that we would figure out that it was a terrible habit to have. Or, maybe she figured that after the novelty wore off we would figure out that it wasn't all it was cracked up to be, and that we would get it out of our system. Whatever the case may have been, it worked. None of us became smokers.

My grandmother passed away when I was about four or five. I have a very vague memory of her passing on, but I do remember Tia Dora being there, comforting her, until the very end. A few years later when my grandfather passed away, it was the same thing. Tia Dora never left his side. Never once did she think of herself. Everything she did was for them. Her life revolved around caring for her parents; she spent her time, efforts, and youth caring for them in total devotion.

Shortly after my grandfather passed away, Tia Dora moved in with us. Instead of taking time for herself and enjoying some of the things that she had missed while she was caring for her parents, Tia Dora decided to help my parents raise us. Being there are eight of us, that was no small task. She went everywhere with us. When we went shopping, she came along to help us keep up with Dad. She did her best to make sure we didn't get lost or left behind. I remember hearing her say, "Vamonos, tu Pappi ya se largo a otra tienda." – "Let's go, your Dad already left to another store." And we'd all run out chasing Dad. Tia Dora would follow behind us helping us keep up with Dad's pace. We'd all laugh, because as soon as we'd all finally make it to the next store, Dad was already on his way out. Tia Dora would start yelling again, "Vamonos, vamonos" as she'd be the last one out of the store.

When my oldest brother P.J. and my sister Mimi were learning how to drive, Tia Dora took the time to teach them. She used to tell us all these funny childhood stories about her, Dad, and the rest of my tias and tios. Her face would light up as she re-enacted their pasts. I learned a lot of family history through her stories and they're still very dear to my heart.

Even though there was no need for her to do so, she worked as a maid for a few of the wealthier families in our town. She was so accustomed to taking care of someone that she seemed unhappy otherwise. Dad would argue with her that he would provide her with anything she needed and she no longer needed to work. He wanted her to enjoy life and to do whatever she wanted. She responded, "This is what I want to do." I guess it gave her a sense of independence. She was used to caring for someone, and not used to having someone look after her. No matter how much Dad wanted her to relax so that he could tend to her for a change, she stood her ground and kept her jobs. Though she worked for what seemed to be pennies, Tia Dora always seemed to have money. When she sent us to the store for some groceries, she would always give us extra for candy or whatever we wanted. She would never ask for her change. During the time when we were going through some very difficult financial problems, Tia Dora always gave us what little she had. On top of that, ever stern in her Christian belief, she tithed. If the church

was selling raffle tickets, she would always
buy some.

She supported us in everything we did.
Whether it was a bake sale or if we were selling
candy for a school club, she always helped out. I
was once in a bike-a-thon for the March of
Dimes and needed sponsors and Tia Dora helped
me out. I can't remember her ever scolding me
for something I did wrong, but I can remember
her praising me for the things I did right.

Some time later, her sister Tia Lile got very
ill. Tia Dora, without batting an eye, decided to
move in with Tia Lile and help with her sons, my
cousins Johnny and Martin. Tia Lile's health was
like a roller coaster, great some days and bad the
next. For many years, she constantly battled
high blood pressure and diabetes. She developed
a problem with her feet that limited her mobility;
and, due to the severity of her diabetes, her doctor did not want to operate out of fear that she
would not heal. Eventually, Tia Lile was confined
to a wheelchair. Tia Dora helped with chores
around the house and with whatever Tia Lile
needed. Eventually, Tia Lile lost her battle with
these diseases, and she passed away a couple of
years ago. Tia Dora, as always, was by her side
until the end.

Even though Johnny and Martin offered to
take Tia Dora into their homes, Tia Dora moved
back to Mom and Dad's house. Some time later,
not too long ago, she finally decided to retire

from her other jobs. During her tenure as a maid, she not only helped my parents raise us, and Tia Lile raise my cousins, she also helped one of the couples she worked for raise their three children. The youngest, Mitchell, who considers Tia Dora as his second mother, still visits her and gives her a big hug and kiss on the cheek every time he sees her. After coming home from college this past Christmas, Mitchell came by Mom and Dad's house to visit with her and give her a present. It was a thrill for me to see Tia Dora get so excited to see him, and to see Mitchell as a fine young man where a young boy once stood and see in his eyes the genuine love he felt for Tia Dora as they embraced.

I am not sure whether you have seen your guardian angel or not, or if you even believe they exist. Nor am I trying to sway you in one way or the other. I just wanted to tell you my story of a simple and lovely lady who was placed here by the Almighty himself to look after my family and me. You see, Tia Dora always put us before herself. She was determined to do everything in her power to help us, guide us, and protect us. As you can probably tell, Tia Dora never married. Its not that she didn't want to, or that she didn't have an opportunity to; it's just that she felt more compelled to look after her family and friends. Although she never had children, she treated us as if we were her own. Her contributions to our family can never be measured or repaid.

Tia Dora is a living symbol of everything that is pure and right with the world. If she isn't a guardian angel I don't know what or who is, and I don't think it was just a coincidence that she was born on Christmas either. Now, as I see her in the twilight of her years, it's hard for me to imagine what my life would have been or will be without her.

Thank you, Tia Dora, for being an inspiration in my life. Most of all, thank you for being my guardian angel.

Bull's Eye

4-12-'97

It was the Christmas I got a BB gun. I
could not believe it. My own BB gun. I was a big
kid now. No sir, no more little stuff for this guy, I
had a bike and a BB gun, and I was living high
on the hog. Yes sir, I was pretty darn proud of
my graduation from little kid into the big boys.
Now, when my brothers and the other older kids
in the neighborhood went hunting, I would get to
go as one of the hunters and not one of the
flunkies without a gun, constantly begging their
older brothers to borrow their gun. I hated that,
but now it was all over. No more having to plead
for one shot. I had my own gun.

Before, when we would go hunting, I would
just be one of the pack, waiting for one of my
brothers to have pity on me and lend me his
gun. My brother Manny was usually the one that
would let me shoot his gun every once in a
while. I remember my brother Mark would usually lead us all through the back dirt roads of
our neighborhood. We would all walk like sol-
diers into battle, looking every direction. We
would look up into the trees, down on the fields,
and sideways on the fences. There was a dirt
road that was lined with palm trees on both
sides we loved to go to because there were usually pigeons there. We would all walk single file
with my brother Mark in the front. He would
turn around and signal us to be quiet. When he

23

would see a flock of pigeons, or even just one, coming he would call out in a loud whisper, "DUCK!" Everybody would squat and hide.

Of course, when I first started hunting with them, it took me a while to understand just what he meant by that. Every time he said, "DUCK!" I would start looking for a duck. I really thought he meant that he had seen a duck. I can remember thinking to myself "A duck? Wow! This is going to be cool. He's going to kill a duck." I'd be the only one standing as they'd all be telling me to get down. After a few times of hearing "DUCK!" and then everybody telling me to squat, I realized that he hadn't seen a duck and it was his signal for us to hide.

Of all of us in our neighborhood that went hunting, Ramon was one of the better shots. Ramon had a younger brother named Jesse that we all called Chuy. Chuy and I were about the same age. A couple of days after Christmas I went over to Chuy's house to show off my new piece of iron. It was a beautiful Daisy BB gun. Chuy really liked my gun. Both of us took turns at shooting it. I remember telling him the next time we went hunting, he and I would share it and alternate shooting until he got his own. After all, I knew how dangerous it was to be in the pack without a gun to defend yourself.

After a while, Ramon came out of the house and asked us what we were doing. Chuy turned around and showed Ramon my gun. "Look at what Johnny got for Christmas!"

"Wow! That's a nice gun," said Ramon. "Would you mind if I shoot it?"

"Of course not, go right ahead," I answered with a swollen chest full of pride. He started shooting at different things like rocks, cans, and sticks - never missing. I was all excited because they were drooling all over "my" gun. Just then, Chuy grabbed a small box of laundry detergent and headed out to the middle of the vacant field next to their house. He stopped and turned around at about thirty yards or so and held out the small box at arm's length and yelled back, "Ramon, shoot at the box."

Of course Ramon told him no, but Chuy just kept on yelling, "Come on, Ramon, shoot at the box."

"No! I'll end up hitting you instead."

But Chuy would not stop asking. He was like the pesky fly at a family picnic. After about the twelfth or fifteenth time Chuy asked, Ramon finally gave in. He yelled back at Chuy and said, "Okay! But hold it straight out, and whatever you do, DON'T MOVE!"

Ramon cocked the gun and pulled it to his shoulder. Chuy looked like a one armed scarecrow in the middle of the field. Ramon yelled out one more time, "DON'T MOVE!"

He took aim, and "BANG!" he shot the gun - a split second later – THUD - he hit his target.

All I saw was Chuy dropping the box and yelling "OUCH! You hit me on my thumb, you Blankety Blank Blank. I'm going to kill you!"

Ramon yelled back, "I told you I would hit you, but you wouldn't listen to me."

Chuy picked up the box of laundry detergent and started chasing Ramon all over the yard while tears of pain rolled down his face. Ramon beseeched him to stop, but as persistent as Chuy was for Ramon to shoot, he was more intent on getting revenge.

Ramon, older, was faster, and Chuy began to tire. With one last gasp, knowing he wouldn't catch Ramon on the run, he reared back and threw the box of detergent at Ramon. To me, it all seemed to happen in slow motion. The box flew through the air and Ramon wasn't looking back. Ramon, fast as he was, was no match for the speeding box of laundry detergent. It hit Ramon in the back of the neck - "POOF" - detergent flew everywhere. Ramon was covered with white powder, and all of a sudden Chuy's vengeance turned into satisfaction and laughter. I couldn't help but laugh myself as Ramon was covered with soap. He looked funny with his hair all white. Of course it did not take long for Chuy's satisfaction to turn into fear after he realized what he had done to his older brother who was about twice his size. Chuy yelled, "I'm sorry!" and ran inside the house. Ramon handed me back my gun and said, "It's a nice gun, Johnny," and ran in after Chuy. I don't know what Ramon did to Chuy after that because I did not stick around long enough to find out.

As we continued on our hunting quests for birds, lizards, and even locusts, I no longer went unarmed; I was considered one of the hunters. As for Ramon and Chuy, as all brothers should do, they forgave each other. As the years passed by and we all got older, our hunting posses got smaller and smaller until eventually we all stopped. But the memories of those days gone by with my brothers and me will always be embedded down deep in my heart.

Put Me In, Coach

One of the things that I remember most about growing up is my love for baseball. Growing up a small and skinny child, I really did not have much of a chance at most sports. But baseball, there was a sport that did not require a massive build and strength or a lot of height. It did not require you to be the fastest or the strongest, but it did require some smarts, some athleticism, some hand-to-eye coordination, and some savvy cunningness. It was the perfect sport for a runt of the litter such as myself. Being small, I had a low center of gravity and good general coordination. Yup! This was my sport and I loved it. On the field I belonged with the tall and big, with the quick and fast, and with the strong, and in my case, the weak.

The year was 1975, and it was the summer that I was ten. Our coach was the big star running back for our high school. His younger brother was the big star receiver and also sort of his assistant coach. He would only show up when our regular coach couldn't come. I played for the Donna Little League Braves. I was so excited because I knew the great Hank Aaron played for the Braves. Unfortunately for my team, they were stuck with me. You see, the previous year my two older brothers, Manny and Eli, and I went to the tryouts, and they selected Manny and Eli. Since I was their brother, I came along for the ride because one of the league rules was, "If you selected a player that has a brother, you have to take the other brother." That was because you were not supposed to split up family. So, even though Manny did not return because of age, and Eli decided baseball was not for him, I got to come back as a return player, one that was already on the team. Once you were on the team they couldn't get rid of you unless you quit, and there was no chance of me quitting. Are you kidding? Me, quit the game I loved, the only sport I had a chance to actually play? No way!

My problem was our town was so small that they had to combine the eleven- and twelve-year-old kids with the nine- and ten-year-old kids. I was only ten and I was going to have to compete with kids that were eleven and twelve. When you are ten, eleven and twelve seems so much older; besides, the skill and coordination level of an eleven or twelve-year- old is much higher than that of a ten-year-old.

We didn't have any nine-year-olds on our team, and two other friends of mine and I were the only ten-year-olds. They got on the team the same way that I did; they got drafted right along with their older brothers. Needless to say, we were the benchwarmers every game. We got to play when one of two things happened - when our team was way ahead, or when we were way behind - and that was it. But my friends and I were there for every practice and we faced every game with the same enthusiasm that this was finally going to be the game that coach was going to let us play. We did not care when, or in what position, we just wanted to play.

Well, one day our dreams came true... sort of. Remember, I said baseball was a game of savvy and cunning. On this fine summer evening our coach couldn't make the game, so he sent his younger brother in his place. His brother, the assistant coach, would occasionally go to our practices, but had yet to make it to an actual game. He arrived with the regular line-up and batting order and proceeded as planned. As usual, my friends and I were in the corner of the dugout warming the bench with the eager and unlikely anticipation of playing. I couldn't take it anymore so I devised a plan. I didn't tell anyone of my plan for fear of getting caught.

This plan was so crazy and so cunning that I almost talked myself out of it. But this was it. I'd had enough. I wasn't going to sit on the bench any longer. I took control of my own destiny and grabbed the proverbial bull by his horns. I got up during the fourth inning as our defense made the last out at the top of the inning, approached the assistant coach, and calmly said, "You know, coach usually puts me in right about now."

He turned to me and said, "Really," and I said, "Yeah, he usually puts me in right field because hardly anybody hits over there."

Then he said the words that stunned me, "Well, okay then, get ready to go in when we go back in the field."

Even though it shocked the heck out of me on how easy it was, I acted as if that were the norm. I went and got my glove and a ball so I could warm-up, but before I knew it we had gone "three up three down." I trotted out into the field like I knew what I was doing, and all of my teammates - especially my ten-year-old com-rades - were staring at me in amazement. All the while, I was shaking in my shoes and praying they didn't hit the ball my way. I must have said a thousand Our Father's and Hail Mary's.

Then the center fielder yelled out to me, "You better get ready, Mora, because this guy always hits over there."

Great! That's just what I needed. I remem-ber thinking, "Oh, my God, what did I get myself into?" I couldn't stand still. My legs were shak-ing, I was walking in place and I didn't even know it. The lights were bright and the field seemed huge. It felt like I was a mile away from the infield and the centerfielder. That was just too much ground to cover, I could never do that. At first I thought of telling the assistant coach that I was lying and that it was all a joke and to get me out of there, but it was to late.

"Play Ball!" roared the umpire, and the first batter stepped up to the plate.

"Please, God, don't let him hit it this way. I promise I'll never lie again." I begged and pleaded, but to no avail.

"CRACK!" went the sound of the bat that sounded like a cannon.

"Please don't hit it to me, OH MY GOD HE HIT IT TO ME!"

He hit it deep. The center fielder yelled, "BACK!" and with all the speed I could muster I ran towards the fence. I tried not to take my eyes off the ball, just like my brothers had taught me, but I lost it in the lights, and before I knew it I had over ran the ball. I quickly stopped and came back to the ball once I caught sight of it again. I stretched out my glove and the ball hit the palm of my glove and bounced straight up and out of my glove.

I reached out with my bare hand and caught it barehanded.

I remember the umpire yelling, "You're out!" and hearing my family, especially my sisters, yelling above the crowd.

My sister Mimi yelled, "Way to go, Johnny! That's my baby brother!" My family would go to every game even though they knew I wasn't likely to play.

After that first catch I seemed to settle down and started playing like I knew I could. We made the three outs and I rushed back to the dugout. Everybody told me how good a catch I'd made. I felt like part of the team for the very first time that year. My other ten-year-old comrades asked me how I got to play. After I explained my little plan, only one of them had the courage to try the same thing. Wouldn't you know he got put in the game the next inning?

But before we went back out on defense, I had to bat. I got to the on-deck circle and - just before I went up to the batter's box - the coach came to me and said, "Hey Johnny, just squat. You're so small that your strike zone is practically nothing, so just squat, okay?"

"Okay," I said, sort of disappointed. I knew, or just had a feeling, that I could hit the ball. My first time in the big leagues, with the big boys, in a close game, and the coach wanted me to squat. What kind of deal was that?

Oh, well, I stepped up to the plate with the largest bat I could find and lucky, or unlucky, for me I didn't have to squat. The pitcher was so wild that I didn't have time to squat. I ducked, I fell to the ground, and hell, I even had to jump up so that the ball wouldn't hit my feet. I got on base with a walk. Not bad for a little guy who was more used to sitting on the bench than rounding the bases. I didn't get to score, but that didn't dampen my spirits because I got to go back out on defense. As we rushed back out on the field, out came my buddy with the goofiest smile I'd ever seen, like a kid in a candy store. He trotted out to center field. He asked me, "What do I do?"

Me, being the experienced field general that I was, gladly directed him like my teammates had directed me, "You better get ready because this guy always hits that way!"

I could see the same fear in his eyes that I'd just had a few minutes before. He was moving around like he was lost and he started to back up towards the fence when all of a sudden we heard the sound of the bat. "CRACK!" It was a high fly ball to center field. My buddy panicked and didn't move. I started sprinting towards him and yelled, "UP! UP! UP!"... but he just stood there with that deer-in-the-headlights look.

I kept running as hard and as fast as I could towards the ball. Then, so did he. He yelled to me, "I can't see it in the lights."

I yelled back, "I got it!"

And I snagged it right in front of his face.

Again, the crowd and my family went wild. "Great catch Johnny!" yelled the coach. I trotted back to right field like a gazelle. I was floating on air that night. The next batter came up and hit a deep fly ball to me. With all the confidence in the world now, I gave chase to it and caught it right next to the rightfield fence. I was on fire!

The next batter came up and hit a line drive shot right down the rightfield line. I chased it and managed to put a glove on it as it hit the chalk line, but I bobbled it and he got a double.

The next batter came up and hit a hard grounder to second base. I started to charge to cover the second baseman. The runner on second took off; the ball bounced off of the second baseman's foot and passed him as the runner rounded third. The third base coach waved him in as I snagged the ball out of the air after the hop. Then, in one motion, I planted and threw as hard as I could to home plate. I got it there on one hop and the catcher tagged the runner. "YOU'RE OUT!" yelled the umpire.

I felt a rush of electricity go through my body. Everybody high-fived me and congratulated me. I felt ten feet tall and like a hero that night. I got on base every time I went to bat, and I didn't have to squat, either.

Well, my glory was short lived after our real coach came back and gave me an earful about lying to his brother, and how things would have been different if I hadn't gotten lucky the night before. Even though I did get to play more often than my buddies after that night, for the most part it was back to the bench for me. Coach might have taken away the spotlight that was shining on me, but he could never take away that night. That night, I played the best game of my life in baseball.

Years later, when I became a coach, it was those Little League memories, and the coaching philosophies I learned from my brother P.J. when he coached me in Pony League, that compelled me not to let a kid sit on the bench. Not to neglect them because of their age, size or abilities. So I gave to them what I seldom got in little league and so desperately wanted and needed... a chance. A chance to play the game that I love.

None, Zero, Knee Fu
Knee Faah

I can remember when I was growing up in my father's house there were many things we did together as a family. We went to picnics together. We went to church together. We prayed together. We played together. We went to ballgames together, and of all the ballgames that we went together to, none were more exciting than cheering for our local high school football team.

When you grow up in Texas, there are few things taken more seriously than football, and my little hometown of Donna was no different. Football was a thing of tradition. After all, Donna was the only Rio Grande Valley high school that had ever won a state championship back in 1961. Local high school football stars were revered by the kids around town and viewed as icons. I can still remember pretending to run like Keith Fraise, Kim Jackson, or Oscar Guzman, our local heroes. I pretended to catch like Leslie Jackson and to throw like Mitch Kityama. I would pretend to tackle like Mike Wisenbaker or like my brother Manny, who was an absolute terror on the football field. I, like most of the kids in Donna, looked up to those guys and wished to be like them. Unfortunately for me, the good Lord did not give me any athletic ability in most sports, but especially when it came to football, so pretending was about all I could do.

Our Donna Redskins had many rivalries when I was growing up. There were the Weslaco Panthers, the Raymondville Bearkats, the Mercedes Tigers, and the Edcouch-Elsa Yellow Jackets. One of the things I remember most about Friday night football was hurrying to the car after the game and tuning the radio to KGBT AM to hear the colorful comments of all the Rio Grande Valley - a four-county area in the southernmost tip of Texas - high school football scores by Hugo De La Cruz. He would have marching band music blaring as he gave out the scores of the night's games. Hugo usually had nicknames for most of the Valley teams to add more color to his highlights. Of all the teams that he gave nicknames to, none could hold a candle to his hometown Edcouch-Elsa Yellow Jackets. Win or lose, Hugo always showed his allegiance to his Yellow Jackets, or, should I say, his "Tremendous and Potent Yellow Machine" (la Tremenda y Potente Maquina Amarilla) as he called them. When they would win, he would prolong the name and add other snips as his voice would blare "La Tremenda y Potente Maquina Amiriiiiiiiiiiiiillllllllllaaaaaaaa!!!!!" He would repeat it over and over with tremendous excitement as he would add "Derrooooootaaaaa a los Tigeres de Mercedes!!!!!!" Which loosely translates to "Totally Demoooliiiishhhhes the Mercedes Tigers!!!" (or whoever they were playing that week). It didn't matter by how much they won. It could be as little as a field goal or as much as a few touchdowns, the lead into the score was all the same.

It was always great when one team would shut out another because that was when he would add his signature call to the score. "Ni Fu Ni Fa" was his signature call for zero. If the score was Donna Redskins 14 – Weslaco Panthers 0, Hugo would say something like this, "Los Indios Bomberos de Donna 14 y los Panteras de Weslaco NiiiiiiiiiiiFuuuuuu NiiiiiiiiiiFaaaaaa!!!!!! He always called the Donna Redskins "los Indios Bomberos de Donna," which translates to "the Donna Redskin Firemen." I'm not sure what that meant exactly, but that was our nickname.

The fun part of listening to Hugo's show was that he would allow people to call in and request that he play a ballad for their team or certain recordings like a crying baby for the loosing team on behalf of the winning team. It was always funny to hear the people call in, all riled up because someone played the crying baby for their team. You could hear people that were drunk call in and get mad on the air or to clarify that the refs had cheated their team and that was why they had lost.

Of all the people that called him, Rogelio Botello Rios - also a radio personality for the same station - was my favorite. Rogelio, from Donna and a rival to Edcouch-Elsa, would call in and give his two cents in defense and support of the Redskins. It was always better when both Edcouch-Elsa and Donna had good teams and would be heading into what seemed to be a big showdown. Hugo and Rogelio would rib each other about how much better their respective teams were than the other's. Hugo would say that his Tremendous and Potent Yellow Machine was going to demolish the helpless Redskins. Rogelio would call the "Maquina Amarilla" (Yellow Machine) "la maquina de cortar sacate" (the lawnmower). Rogelio would say that the lawnmower was out of gas and that the Redskins were going to scalp them. They would go on and on about the strengths of their teams and jokingly put down the other. When the big game would finally come, it usually made for an exciting game. I hated it when Donna would lose to Edcouch-Elsa because Hugo would croon all night about his "Tremendous and Potent Yellow Machine" beating us. Heaven forbid that they ever held us to zero because then out came the dreaded super extended "NiiiiiiiiiiiiiiiiiiiiiiiFuuuuuuuuuuuuuuuuu NiiiiiiiiiiiiiiiiiiiiiiiFaaaaaaaaaaaaaaaaa!!!!!!!!!!!!!!!" Hugo could hardly contain himself until Rogelio called. When the call finally came, Hugo would brag while Rogelio would have to humble himself to the victor. Fortunately, as I recall, Donna beat Edcouch-Elsa much more than the other way around. To his credit though, Hugo would eat crow and humble himself to Rogelio's bragging when he called in. And he would do it in his usual style and dignity.

As I look back to my childhood now as a grown man and many miles away from home, I smile at how simple life seemed back then. Small towns, good people, good friends, and family outings, a time when it was still safe to be a kid and the word *family* was something special. Friday night football meant hometown heroes could be found grinding it out on the gridiron, as the heroes of the future watched with dreams in their eyes, while the past heroes relived their glory days. It also meant seeing the pride in my parent's eyes every time my brother Manny took the field as one of the local heroes. In the back of my mind, I can still hear the Mighty Redskin Band playing our traditional warpath song as our team marched down the field to score or to help the defense tighten up to stop the opponent.

Most of all, Friday night football meant Hugo De La Cruz and his crazy recap of all the game scores in which he captured the hearts and ears of the Rio Grande Valley. No one else can capture the spirited frenzy that is Friday Night High School Football in South Texas like Hugo can. He's able to take all the fanaticism and wrap it into an electrifying show that is filled with lots of opinions and humor, and every time I go back to the Valley during high school football season, I make sure to tune in his show. His show is definitely a one-of-a-kind, and there is nothing like it or that even comes close. Nope, nothing, none, zero, or as in Hugo's own words: "NiiiiiiiiiiiiiiiiiiiFuuuuuuuuuuuu NiiiiiiiiiiiiiiiiiiiFaaaaaaaaaaaa!!"

The Drive Thru

4-30-'97

One of the things I remember about growing up in my father's house is working for my father at his brick yard. Dad owned a small brick and tile distributorship in Donna, and my four older brothers and I worked for Dad. Well, let me clarify that: we all showed up at his place of business and gave Dad a hard time about working.

When Dad first started his brick and tile business, it was only as a side job to his savings and loan company. When he would get brick orders, we would do all the labor and make all the deliveries. I can still remember Dad coming into the house and telling us that we had to deliver and unload a truck full of brick; the first words out of our mouths were, "How much are we going to get paid?"

If there was one question my Dad hated to hear from us, it was, "How much are we going to get paid?" He would ramble on and on about how he used to work for his dad for free most of the time or how his dad would only pay him a quarter. Of course we never bought those stories, even if they were true.

Eventually Dad started making more money selling brick and tile on the side than he was at the savings and loan, so he sold his share of the savings and loan to his two partners and got into

45

the brick and tile business full-time. At first, he started off with a small office and a big brick-yard. The brickyard behind Dad's office had an oval track about the size of a track around a football field. Trucks with brick from all over would come in on one side of the track, unload, and then leave through the other. Eventually business got better and Dad expanded his office space. He also added a big warehouse in the yard.

During the school year, my brothers and I usually went to Dad's office after school and on Saturday mornings. During the summer, we were there Monday through Friday from eight to five and on Saturdays from eight to noon. Dad had a number of workers and truck drivers who worked from Monday through Friday, but not on Saturday; that was when we were supposed to handle all the work. Of course there usually was not as much work on Saturday as there was during the week. Of all the five boys, only the three youngest of us spent most of our time out-side doing manual labor. Our oldest brother, P.J., was the office manager and our next oldest brother, Mark, did some of the truck driving. That left Manny, Eli, and me to work outside. We worked hard sometimes, but not always. But if you ever heard us complain, it sure sounded like we worked hard all day, everyday.

It was during one of those hot summer months down in south Texas that we were out of school and working for Dad. We never really worked for anybody else back then, except for the time we decided to pick cotton and tomatoes for extra spending money. However, we didn't do that for too long. We found out it was a lot of work for very little money and it really put a strain on our backs.

Dad must have gotten tired of hearing us give him a hard time about how little we were getting paid, because he told us that we were not working hard enough to get paid more. He told us that his regular employees worked harder for him than his own sons. Looking back now, I know that was true. I think I knew then, also, that that was true, but at the time we (or, at least, I) took offense to that. I thought we were working pretty hard. So what if we took longer breaks than the regular workers? So what if we would fall asleep in the conference room during break time and lunch time and overslept most days? I still thought we worked pretty darn hard. I decided I was going to show him. I was going to work harder and faster than ever. I don't know if that was his plan all along; but if it was, it sure worked on me.

I was fired up the next day. I got to work on time and I was ready to work. We started out packing brick and I was working like a finely tuned machine. I cranked out bundles of bricks like they were going out of style. At the time, a bundle of bricks consisted of four hundred and fifty four bricks. I must have put out close to twenty bundles that morning and I don't think I even took a break. After lunch it was back to work. This time we had to bundle brick that were in the very back of the yard. Again, I was like that Energizer bunny - just going and going and going.

Then it hit me. I'd had a big lunch, and I needed to use the restroom. I thought to myself, "I can't slow down now! I have to go and get back quickly."

I figured the fastest way for me to get to the office and back was for me to take the forklift. I got on the forklift and sped off. I had the pedal to the metal and I was hauling. I don't recall what the top speed of our forklift was, but I was definitely doing it. Since you steered it with the rear wheels, it was hard to keep the forklift going straight. As I swerved back and forth and the wind was blowing in my face, all I could think of was, "I have to get back to work as soon as I can."

To the left, as I approached the back of Dad's office, was a row of parked cars that belonged to Dad's workers. Then there was a lane that was just wide enough for the forklift and about 20 yards deep. And to the right of that were stacks of brick bundles.

As I got closer to the back of Dad's office, I turned into the lane and let my foot off the gas. I stepped on the brake and then I remembered something I had forgotten to do.

For the brakes to work, I had to pump them before I took off.

Panic struck me like a ton of bricks, no pun intended, and I didn't know what to do. I started pumping the brakes as fast as I could, but that didn't work. The back wall of Dad's office was coming up fast. I can remember thinking, "Oh, my God! I'm going to die! If the crash doesn't kill me, my father will!"

For a moment I thought of jumping out. I got my bottom off the seat for an instant, but I realized I was too close to the wall, going too fast, and now there was no place for me to jump. I sat back down. I braced myself, holding on to the steering wheel as hard as I could, I clamped my feet down, and waited for the impact.

No sooner had I braced myself than BOOM! I hit the wall with the forks in the air.

The jolt threw me off my seat and onto the steering wheel. The whole office shook with the impact. One of the forks hit the middle of one of the cinder blocks on the wall and went clear through to the inside. The other fork hit the mortar joint between two cinder blocks and pushed both of them in. I remember the crash hurting like a son of a gun and knocking the wind out of me, but I was so shocked and scared of what Dad was going to do to me, I pretended to be okay.

I backed the forklift out from the wall, got off, and ran back to work. I completely forgot about going to the restroom, but if you ask my brothers they would tell you that I did it in my pants. I was sure Dad was going to kill me. This was it; I was in big trouble.

Dad didn't even have to ask, he knew it was me. The funniest thing was that Dad hardly even yelled at me. What was embarrassing was that he didn't fix the holes in the wall until one or two years later. Believe me, that - coupled with my brothers and Dad's workers ribbing me - was more than punishment enough.

Looking back now I see a couple of things I could've done to avoid the crash. None of that matters now. What matters are the lessons that Dad was trying to teach us. He taught us the value of money and how hard it was to make. He taught us to never back down from a hard and honest day's work. He taught us that there was nothing wrong with being a laborer, and to always take pride in what you do, because how you feel about your job reflects in how well you do it. He also taught us that, if we did not want to be laborers for the rest of our lives, education was the way to go. He always said, "They can take away your house, your car, your money and all your belongings, but they can't take away your education. As long as you have that, you will always have a solid foundation to start all over again and reclaim all that was taken away from you."

Strong words from a strong man who knew what it was like to have everything taken away from him and getting it all back.

Although I value the education that I received in school, I know that the education that my father gave me was of far greater influence and importance in my life.

Dad, as is the case with most parents, always wanted us to have more than he ever could have had. He sacrificed himself and paved the way so we could expand our horizons and achieve the things he could not. And as I stand on the frontier of my horizons, on the road that Dad paved for me, ready to expand it for the generation that follows me, I can't help but look back at the road my father built for me to help me achieve my dreams, the wonderful road that he paved with bricks.

Thanks, Dad. I love you.

Those Blessed Shoes

---------- *12-14-'96* ----------

I have many fond memories of things that happened between Dad and me while I was growing up. Some of them serious, some of them embarrassing, some of them funny; all of them special.

One of the things Dad has always done in my life is instill a solid foundation and a belief in Christ. My parents, devout Catholics and Christians, made sure we did not stray too far from our upbringing. They made sure we were involved in as many activities our parish had to offer. Dad was always involved in so many activities in our parish that often his responsibilities trickled down to us, his children. We were always at church when we were kids and everybody knew he was our dad. He got us into the altar boys. When the church had any kind of festival we were there setting up the hall for it. When the festival was over we were there cleaning it up afterwards. Since Thursday night was bingo night, we were there helping in the concession stand. Of course we would also play bingo - we were not without our fun. He made us go to retreats and bible studies. I can remember people calling Dad at all hours to see if he would come and pray a rosary for a sick family member or at a funeral. Heck, he even taught some of my older brothers and sisters in C.C.D. (Confraternal Christian Doctrine, Sunday School for Catholics). Needless to say, we had a reputation to live up to.

Being Catholic, Dad was always blessing things: our meals, our trips (even short ones like to the grocery store), and, of course, us. I can still remember him coming into our room at night and blessing us while we were pretending to sleep. Even when we were older, he would come in and give us his blessing. He had our priest come over and bless our house once because we (my brothers and I) thought we had heard voices in the middle of the night. Blessings were a big thing in our house.

When Dad was not at church or chewing us out for terrorizing our sisters, he was at work. And when we were not in school, at church, or terrorizing our sisters, we were with him at work. And just like at home, Dad would bless the business too. Every morning, like a ritual, he would take a glass of holy water and go to the back door and with his eyes closed he would open the door, and in small pours, of water he would make a cross on the ground just outside the door. He would then turn and go to the front door and do the same. In the evening before he left, it was the same thing all over again. I knew, we all knew, that he did this like clockwork.

One Saturday morning when I was in high school, I arrived at Dad's office earlier than normal. Because my brothers and I were always late, I was there before them. I can still remember being half asleep and stumbling to the front door of the office. As I reached for the door knob, to my surprise, Dad opened the door with his eyes closed and poured holy water all over my shoes and gave them a blessing. He startled me and I tried jumping out of the way. Unfortunately, he was too quick with the holy water. Dad was surprised when he opened his eyes and saw me standing there with my shoes soaking wet. He had a dazed look in his eyes and for a moment it looked as if he thought that I had appeared out of thin air. After our initial shock, he realized that he had blessed my shoes and not the entryway to the office and said, "I'm sorry son, I didn't see you standing there." We both sort of laughed it off and went in only, of course, after he made me move so that he could bless the entrance one more time just to be sure.

I don't recall just what exactly happened to those shoes. I can only assume they are waiting for me in the afterlife as my only pair of shoes that were ever blessed. As I tuck my son into bed at night and I give him a little blessing with the sign of the cross on his little forehead, I hope he feels as safe, loved, and protected as I did when Dad did the same for me.

Thanks, Dad, for all those blessings.

The Auction

———— *4-12-'96* ————

As I sit here and look back at some of the crazy and ignorant things that I have done in my life, I recall the first and last auto auction I ever attended. I had just moved back to Donna after a five-year absence to work in Houston and Austin. After being laid off three times in five years and moving from big city to big city, I had finally found a decent job with a lot of security. I went to work for the State of Texas. It was almost perfect. The job was in a small town just ten minutes from my hometown. It was close enough for me to drive home for lunch, where Mom would have fresh homemade food ready and hot just for me. I didn't have to worry about being laid off because it was a state job. I mean, you would have to mess up pretty bad to get let go by the state.

Most of my family was still close to home, which made visiting a lot easier and nicer. The only drawback was that my fiancé, Rode, was still in college and living in Austin. Instead of me making frequent trips from Austin to Donna to visit my family, I had to make the same trip in the opposite direction to visit Rode. But, since we grew up relatively close to each other, we decided that after she graduated we would get married and live somewhere between our hometowns.

One day at work my buddies raved about this great place where auto auctions were held every Tuesday night. Being that this place was in Donna, they asked me if I'd ever been to one. I just said no, but I didn't go into detail about my personal reasons for not going.

You see, at one time Dad was the proud owner of a brick and tile distributorship in my hometown. After many years of good business, the economy seemed to drop with no warning, and - since we lived close to the border - when the peso devaluation hit, it was like the proverbial straw that broke the camel's back. Dad had to file for bankruptcy, and we lost almost everything. The business that Dad built from nothing was gone, and this great auction site my friends were talking about was the same exact place where Dad had his business. Even though the auction place had no fault in my father's demise, every time I passed it by, it boiled my blood.

It was very painful and emotional for me, but after seeing the feverish look in my friends' eyes when they spoke of this place, it caught my curiosity. I fought back my emotions and personal anguish and inquired about all the details of what exactly went on at this place. I found out what time the auction started, what time you could inspect the cars that were going to be auctioned that night, and how the payment plans worked. The auction started at seven p.m. sharp. You could arrive as early as five o'clock to inspect the cars, and payment was normally due on the spot after the sale, but - with twenty percent down - they would give you until ten o'clock the next morning to pay. Cash only, absolutely no checks accepted.

My friends warned me that it was easy to get caught up in the bidding, but I didn't believe them. I didn't tell them that the real reason I was going for was so I could visit Dad's old office and reminisce the days when I was growing up and working for Dad.

At five o'clock I left work and rushed home. I changed into some shorts and a T-shirt, put on some sneakers, and I was off. I drove to the auction place, recalling the days of when it was Dad's business.

My emotions were going crazy. It had been about nine years since I had last been to this place, and I was a bit on edge.

I finally arrived at the famed auction place, and as I walked through the door of the main building, it was like I was walking through a time zone. All of a sudden I was a teenager in Dad's office building. On the walls were a variety of brick and tile samples. On the far back wall were the two holes I had made when I drove Dad's forklift through the wall. On the desks and on the counters were letter heads, business cards, pens and pencils all with "Mora Brick and Tile" written all over them. I walked out of the main building and into the back yard where the auctioneer kept all the cars he was going to sell that night. Only I didn't see them. All I saw was rows of bricks stacked high and Dad's eighteen-wheelers lined up waiting to be loaded for a delivery to Houston or a neighboring city.

I spotted the warehouse where we kept the entire stock of tile and the machinery that Dad owned to run a first-class brick and tile operation. Heck, we even stored the forklift in there. Only now it was filled with auto parts and it had a bunch of desks and files where they kept records of all the cars they were going to sell that night. Beside those regular desks was a towering desk/judge's bench/pulpit - looking thing with what looked like a blue light that had been taken off of a police squad car, with a string to turn it off and on like a lamp next to it. I didn't know what it was for, but as I found out later, it definitely had its purpose.

I spent most of my time remembering the old days, and before I knew it the auction started. When you first came in they handed you a ticket, like a movie ticket stub, and being the pack rat that I am I put it in my pocket. They rolled out the first car, and on top of the immense desk sat a loud white-haired auctioneer. He started off in his auctioneer's jargon that I didn't understand and all of a sudden he yelled, "Sold! To the man in the red cap."

No sooner than they rolled out the sold car, they rolled in a new car. The auctioneer started

off again, and again the car was sold before I
could tell what was going on.

As the night progressed I started getting
into the whole mumbo-jumbo and understanding
what was going on. They rolled in another car
and the auctioneer took off, "Let's start the bidding at fifteen hundred dollars." The man next to
me raised his hand.

"Do I hear sixteen hundred?" A lady across
the way nodded.

The bidding went all the way up to thirty-
four hundred dollars and stopped, and the auctioneer wailed, "Do I hear thirty-five? Thirty-
five? Do I hear thirty-four fifty? Thirty-four
fifty?" Just then he reached over and yanked on
the cord of that blue squad car light. It turned
on and strobed like a cop's bright blue light
when you've been speeding.

He grabbed the microphone and said, "Every
time I turn this blue light on, it means that the
car has no minimum bid on it and it will sell to
the highest bidder." Some owners would put a
minimum bid on their cars, and they would not
sell unless that minimum bid was met. "Do I
hear thirty-four twenty-five? Thirty-four twenty-
five? Thirty-four twenty-five going once, going
twice, sold! For thirty-four hundred dollars to
the man in the blue shirt."

By this time, just standing there and not doing anything was boring me. So, against my better judgement, I started bidding right along with every one else. At first I started slow. I was usually one of the early bidders. Then I would stop after the bidding got higher and I knew I was going to get out-bid. Every time I bid it gave me a shot of adrenaline and my blood would rush through my veins like a race car in the Indy 500. My heart would start beating faster and faster, a sort of fear and thrill at the same time.

I thought to myself, "Man, this is fun." I really got into it. I would nod my head, I would raise my hand, and I would pull on my ear, and one time I even winked at the guy. Needless to say, I was letting things get out of control, but I was hooked like a smoker to nicotine. I felt like a junkie waiting for his next fix to get high. I was no longer listening to my common sense. Instead, I was flying solo and by the seat of my pants. I was bidding on anything and every-thing. I even bid on a huge van that could carry a classroom full of kids to a field trip.

They rolled out this big Buick station wagon that looked like the family truckster from National Lampoon's "Family Vacation" and I was about to start bidding when an elderly man and what seemed to be his daughter came and stood beside me.

"There it is!" she said excitedly, all glassy-eyed like a kid at a pet shop window. "I've been waiting for it all night. I sure do hope we get it. Do you think we can?" she turned and asked her dad.

"Well I'll give it my best shot." How much did you say you had?" he asked.

"Two thousand, five hundred. Do you think that's enough?"

"I don't know. We'll find out soon enough."

The auctioneer got going, "Let's start the bidding at fifteen hundred."

The proud dad raised his hand first.

"Do I hear sixteen?"

Someone yelled, "here!"

"Do I hear seventeen?"

Before the dad could raise his hand, another man on the other side of me raised his cap.

"Do I hear eighteen?"

This time, leaving no room for doubt, the dad yelled out, "Over here!"

I was really pulling for the dad and daughter next to me, but the bidding seemed to be going too fast and her budget was coming around the corner faster than a thoroughbred at the Kentucky Derby. Every time the man on the other side of me would bid, I would give him a mean stare, but he never got the hint nor felt the wrath of my glare and continued bidding.

I looked him up and down. He looked like a used car salesman, just there to find another car for his lot. He didn't need that station wagon like this poor father and daughter next to me. Every time the dad would bid his daughter's eyes would light up like firecrackers. Every time someone else would bid, she would get a worried look in her face.

The bidding got to twenty-four hundred dollars faster than the man of steel himself. It didn't look good.

"Do I hear twenty-five hundred?" The dad let out a resounding, "HERE!" out of desperation, but to no avail.

"Do I hear twenty-six hundred?" The used car salesman raised his stupid red cap again.

The daughter, with her face filled with disappointment, hung her head in utter disbelief. How could life be so cruel to her?

Her dad threw his arms around her, embraced her and said, "It's going to be O.K."

"Do I hear twenty-seven hundred?" wailed the auctioneer.

Then, out of nowhere, the dad raised his right arm and yelled, "Over here!"

The daughter's head popped straight up, her eyes burst wide open while shaking her head and saying, "No! You can't do this."

"Yes I can. I have some money put away for something just like this."

Again she said, "No! I won't let you."

"It's too late." said the dad, "I already did."

The bidding started to slow down and it was down to just the dad and that mangy used car salesman with the red cap.

The dad put up a good fight and I could tell he was already stretching his budget by the scared look in his eye. Then, the inevitable came: the dad could no longer continue.

It seemed like that dirty, no good, rotten scoundrel of a used car salesman's pockets were just too deep.

The dad's head fell just like his daughter's.

Embracing each other, they knew it wasn't going to happen. Seeing their misfortune, I felt like bidding against that evildoer and beating him at his own game. I could bid against him and let the dad and the daughter buy the car off of me with the money they already had and then pay the rest of it to me in payments. I didn't have any money, so that was impossible. But I did bid against him a couple of times, just to bring the bid a little higher and make him pay. He ended up paying thirty-seven hundred dollars for that station wagon. I thought justice had been served for not letting that poor dad and daughter have that car. What did I know about justice? I had just bid against a man so he would have to pay more for a car I wasn't going to buy.

They started rolling in nicer cars and there was a stretch where they rolled in five or six Lincoln Town Cars in a row. They were all selling for about forty-five hundred dollars and I was getting all caught up in the bidding again. I bid on every single one. Then they rolled out a big beautiful gray Lincoln Town Car with a black top. It sure looked sharp. The auctioneer got the bid going. "Do I hear thirteen hundred?"

Some lady yelled, "Here!"

"Do I hear fourteen hundred?"

That jerk in the red cap raised it again.

I'll teach him, I thought. I'll make the bid go higher so he can spend more money on it than he wants to.

"Do I hear fifteen hundred?" called the auctioneer.

"Over here!" I yelled as I gave that cur a snooty look.

"Do I hear sixteen hundred?" said the auctioneer and the crowd went deafly quiet. "I said sixteen hundred," the auctioneer called.

Then the totally unexpected happened. The auctioneer turned, reached over, and pulled the cord of the blue squad car light.

He said, "That's right! This baby is going to sell no matter what. There is no minimum bid on this one fellas. Do I hear sixteen hundred?"

Still no noise from the crowd. I looked around. No one seemed interested in the car.

"Come on people, somebody give me sixteen hundred."

Still no answer.

"Do I hear fifteen fifty?"

No answer.

"Fifteen fifty?"

You could hear a pin drop.

"Do I hear fifteen twenty-five?"

By this time, I'm panicking. I turned around and looked at the nice guy in the red cap and gave him my "come on, ol' buddy, ol' pal" look, but it didn't work. He didn't budge.

"Fifteen twenty-five? Going once."

I looked all over, thinking, "Somebody help me out here. Please!"

Nothing.

"Going twice."

Still nothing.

"Sold, to the man in the blue shorts for fifteen hundred dollars! Man you just got yourself a steal."

I didn't know what to do. I didn't have fifteen hundred dollars. Where was I going to get fifteen hundred dollars? For an instant I thought, "I'll just turn around here and make a run for it." Just then, two huge guys came up behind me to make sure that I didn't do exactly that.

"Sir, sir," the auctioneer called out to me, "you need to come up here to this desk to pay for your car."

"Pay for my car!" I thought to myself. "How the heck am I going to do that?" I started walking to the desk knowing I didn't have any cash on me. My heart was racing a hundred miles an hour, my palms were sweating, and my knees were shaking.

I reached the counter and I spotted an old friend of mine from high school behind the desk. She said, "Hi, Johnny. How are you?"

"Not so good," I said with a trembling voice.

"What's the matter?"

"Well, I just bought that car, and I don't have any cash on me to give you. All I have is my checkbook."

"Well, we're not supposed to accept checks, but since I know you, you can pay with a check."

"Thanks. How much do I make it for?"

"Twenty percent would be three hundred dollars."

I think she saw the befuddled look on my face because then she said, "But you can just make it out for one hundred if you want."

That was great. The one hundred I could cover. It was the other fourteen hundred I was going to have a real problem with. So I asked her, "Is there anyway you can give me more time to pay? I don't think I can get the rest of the money to you by ten tomorrow morning."

"I'm sorry. I wish I could, but the auctioneer is real strict on that. He usually doesn't let people do that."

"No problem," I said, "it's okay, I'll see you tomorrow." But it really wasn't okay. I had no idea what I was going to do. In my head, I rushed through a million options. "I'll call Joe at the credit union tomorrow and apply for a signature loan. He's always asking me to take out a loan."

"No, no that won't be any good," I responded to myself. "I'll have to fill out a long application, and there is no way that I'll have the money by ten a.m. Geez! The bank doesn't even open until nine."

What was I going to do?

"I know! I'll call Rode in Austin tonight and explain to her what I'd just done. I'll beg and plead with her to wire me the money, and I'll be able to pay the auctioneer in time." Yeah, yeah that just might work. "That will give me time to go talk to Joe at the credit union and apply for a loan to repay Rode her money."

She had just gotten all her scholarship
money for school and it was all she had.
So I was going to have to get her the money
back fast.

I was still nervous and shaking from my
big blunder. Talk about justice. I sure got
my justice.

I went back and stood at the very same spot
that I was in, but only this time I didn't bid anymore. I just stood there, shocked at what I had
just done. I felt like a total idiot.

I noticed that people were starting to leave.
Just then, the used car salesman turned to me
and asked, "Do you want my tickets?"

"No, thank you." What kind of question was
that? What would I want his tickets for? He
then turned to another guy next to me and
asked him the same question, only that guy
accepted them. He gave him about five tickets.
I saw the guy put them in his shirt pocket. I
went over and asked, "What do you do with
those tickets?"

The guy turned and said, "At the end of the
night, when all the cars have been sold, they give
away a car. They use the numbers on these
tickets to give it away, but you have to be here
for that because if they call a number and no
one claims it, they keep on picking until someone wins."

"That was great!" I thought to myself thinking I could win the car.

Then he added, "And if you want, you can turn around and have them auction it off and get money for it."

That was it! The answer to my problem! All I had to do was win that car - have them auction it off and that would give me enough, or most of the money that I needed for the car I had just purchased. All I had to do was win that car.

So, as I noticed people leaving, I'd ask them to give me their ticket, and most of them obliged. Pretty soon I had about twenty tickets. The last car could not come soon enough for me. Finally, the last car sold. I looked around and there were only twenty or thirty people left. My chances were great. They rolled in a little Ford Escort. It was very nice and very clean. It could very easily sell for the fifteen hundred I owed.

The auctioneer said, "O.K., everybody pull out your tickets. When I call out the winning number, you will have one minute to come and claim the car. If no one claims it within a minute, I'll go on to the next number."

This was it, the moment I was waiting for. I was sure I had the winning number. The auctioneer called out the first number and I looked through each one of my tickets. Darn! I didn't have it! Luckily, neither did anyone else.

He called out the next number, and the next, and the next. He must have called out fifteen to twenty numbers and no one had the winning number. He called out another number. I looked through my tickets, and again I didn't have it.

Then the guy next to me said, "Shit! I forgot that I had stuck these tickets in my shirt pocket."

I saw him get the tickets that the damned used car salesman had offered me, and the guy yelled, "I got it! I got the winning number!"

My heart dropped to the floor. Those were supposed to be my tickets. That salesman offered them to me first. I couldn't believe it. It was like a bad dream, but I was awake. It was really happening and it just kept getting worse. The guy decided to turn around and sell the car. After all was said and done, the car sold for twenty-one hundred dollars. Talk about getting kicked when you're down. I was devastated. I could not believe the chain of events that had unfolded before my very eyes. With my sanity hanging on by mere threads, I drove straight to my parent's house.

After explaining the whole ordeal to my parents, Dad told me he knew the auctioneer and he would talk to him the next day, and try to get me some more time. That was a little relief.

After lots of begging and pleading to Rode, she finally agreed to wire me the money; even though the money didn't get to my bank in time the next day, she made me realize just how lucky I was to have her. All she had to live on was that scholarship money, and she sent it to me anyway. After I got it, though, I sent it right back to her.

Dad talked to the auctioneer and he gave me enough time to borrow the money at the bank. I tried to turn around and sell the car for a small profit, but it just wouldn't sell. I was stuck with it. The harder I tried to sell it, the less people wanted to buy it. It was like I had the plague, and nobody would come near me or the car.

Finally, my brother Eli saved me and said he needed a car to get to and from work and that the Lincoln would be perfect for him. He ended up keeping the car another five years, and when it seemed that every other car in the family was breaking down, that car kept on ticking. After he bought himself a brand new truck, Eli told my parents to sell it for whatever they could get for it. My parents ended up selling it for three hundred bucks.

Ever since that infamous day at the auction, Rode, now my wife, has banned me from all auctions, no matter what they are selling. She says it's just too risky. I can't say I blame her.

Every time I pass a Lincoln Town Car, or one passes me on the street, I remember that day at the auction, and my face turns red with shame and embarrassment, and I have to laugh at myself.

Yes, I have done a lot of dumb things in my life, but the lessons I have learned from those things are priceless. And Rode still loves me.

The Rainbow

9-25-'97

Growing up, I read and heard many times
the Irish legend of "The Pot of Gold at the end of
a Rainbow." This legend explains that lep-
rechauns hide their gold at the foot of the rainbow. Growing up I was always fascinated with
rainbows. I thought they were bold and beautiful, and their mere existence amazed me. First
came the storm and then the rainbow. When
the rainbow came out, you knew the worst of the
storm was over. It was like a sign from God to
me, something to let me know that everything
was going to be okay.

I can remember the day I left my little
hometown of Donna, Texas to move to the big
city of Houston. It was a time of transition for
me and I was excited and scared at the same
time; scared, because I had never been away
from home or on my own before, and excited, for
the challenges that lay before me, to prove
myself and show I belonged.

Three friends of mine from college, Jaime,
Nick, and Armando, and I were going to be moving and rooming together. They were in the
same boat I was: they also hadn't been away
from home or on their own. Somehow, though,
they seemed more secure and ready than I was.

Jaime came by early in the morning to help me load all my belongings in a van he borrowed from his mother's flower shop. I remember my older sister Nita standing on the front sidewalk of Mom and Dad's house. She called out to me, and I thought she was just going to give me a quick hug and tell me goodbye. She actually gave me a HUGE hug as tears ran down her face. She forced some money in my hands, because she knew I didn't have any, and said, "This is for you Johnny. I love you. Please take care of yourself." I was extremely touched and moved, and to this day I can still picture that moment – the warm cloudy morning, with a slight breeze in the air - as if it just happened yesterday.

After my last good-byes to my family, we were off to pick up our friend Nick who lived in Brownsville. As we started out of town, it started to rain cats and dogs. It was pouring so hard that it was difficult to see the road. As if that wasn't bad enough, halfway to Brownsville we had a blowout, and didn't have a spare. We walked about a quarter mile in the rain to the nearest phone and called Nick to come help us. While Nick was on his way, Jaime took the bad tire off the van. Nick picked us up and took the tire and us back to Brownsville to a repair shop. While the tire was being fixed, we went to eat breakfast. By this time the rain had stopped. We finally got our tire back and went to pick up the van, but we had lost valuable time. We had to be in Houston by five p.m. to get our apart-

ment or we would have to spend the night somewhere else, and we still had to pick up Armando
in Sinton, which was about two hours away.
Jaime told me to go with Nick in his car and that
he would follow us in the van.

We finally arrived in Sinton to pick up
Armando, but he wasn't ready. He and his
brothers had been putting a new roof on their
mother's house, and he hadn't even packed. We
waited a little while, and he finally told us to go
on without him, that he would catch up to us in
Houston. So we loaded his big stuff into the
van, and off we went again. We'd lost more valuable time and it was going to be even harder to
make it to Houston by five. Nick told Jaime that
he and I were going ahead of him in his car to
try to make it to Houston in time, and for Jaime
to take his time in the van. Of course, shortly
after we got back on the road, the rain started
again, even harder. Needless to say, Nick could-
n't drive all that much faster than Jaime in the
van. Nick, worried about making it on time,
seemed to stop every forty-five minutes to an
hour to call the apartment complex and tell
them that we were on our way and might be
a little late.

Of course he was killing more time doing
that instead of just driving on at a steady pace.

We kept going and the rain kept coming
down hard, never letting up. As we got closer to
Houston, Nick started going faster. Just as it

looked as if we were going to be able to make it in time, we ran into Houston rush-hour traffic, something we had not considered. It was a quarter to five, the sky was dark and full of lightening, and the rain was still coming down hard, which made traffic even worse.

It took us another two and a half hours to make it to our apartment complex, and by that time it was too late. It was closed and we were going to have to wait until morning to get our key. Thank God Nick's cousin, Eddie, lived in Houston; he let us spend the night with him. Otherwise, we would have had to rent a room somewhere and I certainly didn't have any money other than for my part of the deposit and first month's rent.

We waited for Jaime at the apartment complex to tell him that we didn't make it there on time and we were going to spend the night at Eddie's apartment.

When we went to get some of our clothes out of the van, we discovered the van had a small hole in the back and some water had gotten in. Almost everything in the back of the van had gotten wet, including some of our clothes. Fortunately, it was just a little bit of water and not a lot, so our stuff wasn't too wet.

To me, all of this seemed like an omen. I thought, "Maybe we weren't supposed to come to Houston. If it was this much trouble, maybe the

Lord had other plans for us," but the next morning He gave me His wonderful sign. I saw a big rainbow in the big blue Texas sky, and I knew then that everything was going to be okay.

Some time later, about a year and a half, I got laid off from my job in Houston. Luckily, I found a job in Austin within two weeks. My parents, my oldest brother P.J., and his fiancé Toni came to help me move. We packed Dad's little Dodge/Mitsubishi pickup truck to the gills with most of my stuff; the rest we packed into my little Honda. I had already signed a lease for an apartment in Austin. All I had to do to get the keys was show up, sign some last-minute paper work, and leave a security deposit. Dad brought a big tarp to cover my stuff in the back of the truck, just in case it were to rain on our trip. It was good thinking because shortly out of Houston, the rain came, not real hard, but it came nonetheless. It came and went during most of our trip, until about an hour outside of Austin, when it started to rain hard. The closer we got to Austin, the harder it rained. Soon, it was raining so hard we had to slow down to about twenty miles an hour just to see the road. When we pulled into Bastrop, a little town about thirty miles east of Austin, we could see funnel clouds forming in the sky. Over the radio, the DJ kept breaking in to announce there had been a tornado seen somewhere in Bastrop County and the whole listening area was under a tornado and severe thunderstorm warning.

That didn't help our nerves any. Here we were, barely crawling at twenty miles an hour and this guy is blaring on the radio saying that we were in the middle of a tornado. If a tornado were to hit close by, we wouldn't even be able to see it because the rain was coming down so hard. As it was, we could barely see the hood of our car.

We kept on going through the downpour and made it into Austin without getting hit by a tornado. We found out later that the tornado had passed right by where we drove. When we arrived at the apartment complex, the rain was still coming down in buckets. We got soaked making a dash for the leasing office. When we got there, I asked for Susan, the leasing agent who had helped me when I came to find the apartment. Well, Susan no longer worked there - she had quit the day before.

I told them who I was, that Susan had approved me for an apartment, and that I was there to sign the final paperwork and leave a security deposit to get the key to my apartment. They looked for my application everywhere and couldn't find it. They said I was going to have to fill out another application and wait a couple of days for approval before they could let me have an apartment.

I was steamed and I blew my top. I explained I had just arrived in Austin from Houston and I had no place to stay for a couple of nights. If I had known this would happen, I wouldn't have come all this way with all of my belongings with no place to stay. Besides, Susan told me I had already been approved and all I had to do was show up, sign the final paper-work, leave my deposit, and get the key.

The leasing agent said she was sorry, but there was nothing that she could do. However, she didn't really sound all that sorry. It was more like she was annoyed. I asked to speak to the manager instead. When the manager arrived, I had a few choice words with her as well, then Dad stepped in.

He wasn't as colorful in his speech as I was, but he let them know in a stern manner that this was their mistake, not ours. The manager tried to get out of it, but Dad was too persistent. He kept saying, "We are not leaving here until you apologize to us for your mistake and give us the keys to our apartment." The manager knew she was wrong and finally had to give in.

A while after our success, the rain finally slowed down and we unloaded everything into my new apartment. Of course, everything had gotten soaked from all of the rain; only this time not just a little, but drenched. Again I ques-tioned my decision to move and thought, "Why did I have to go through all this trouble? Maybe the Lord didn't want me to move."

Again he answered me the next day with a great big rainbow in the bright blue Texas sky. I knew then that everything would be okay.

I moved several more times inside the city of Austin, and each time I moved it rained. Not quite as severe as those first two times, but none the less it did. And each time it rained, a rainbow appeared to tell me everything was going to be okay. It got to the point that I expected it to rain every time I moved. Looking back now, it's probably why it did.

Ever since the day I left home, I had dreamed of going back and living again among my family and friends. My wish eventually came true: I got an offer from the Texas Department of Transportation to work close to Donna, my hometown. That was the good news. The bad news was that I had started dating Rode in Austin. So I had a problem: I could go back home, something I had been longing for since the day I left, or I could stay in Austin close to the woman that I was more than sure I was going to marry.

I couldn't make this decision on my own, so I asked Rode what she thought. She, being the trooper that she is, knew what I had always wanted. She asked, "If I was not here, or if you did not know me, would you stay?"

"No," I replied. "Well, then, you should go home. After I graduate from college, I will move back also, and we can get married then."

I know how hard that was for her to say, but she did it for me so that I could live my dream. I will never be able to repay her for that.

We made the decision then - I was going home. Again, I was excited and scared at the same time, excited because I was going home and scared because I didn't want to lose or forsake my relationship with Rode.

It took my family and me several trips to get all my junk back home. I made the last trip by myself because I didn't want my family to see me get all sappy with Rode when we said our last good-byes. In other words, I didn't want them to see me cry as I left her behind. I kept thinking to myself, I'm not leaving her, I'm just moving to another town that was 320 miles away.

I usually kept the radio blaring so I could stay awake when I was alone on trips, but this time I left it off. I was alone, just me and my thoughts. I counted the years that had passed since I left home. Five, it had been five years. I recalled the good times and the bad during those five years. The one good thing that kept jumping out at me was the span of time since I had first met Rode. Before I knew it I was about thirty miles south of San Antonio.

I started questioning myself, "Am I making the right choice? Am I being self-centered?" It was then that I realized, "Hey, it hasn't rained once on my moving trips between Donna and Austin. Is this an omen? Is the Lord trying to tell me something? Where is the rain and where is the rainbow?" I convinced myself I was wrong, that I'd made the wrong choice. I told myself, "If it doesn't rain on this, my last trip, I need to do something to make this right."

Just then it started. At first, a few drops here and there, and then a huge downpour. It started raining so strong cars were pulling over and stopping on the shoulder of the road. I kept going. I was barely crawling and my windshield wipers were going as fast as they could. Then, just as fast as it came, the rain stopped. It had only rained for five or ten minutes, and the clouds and sky remained dark. I thought to myself, "Well, I guess that was the rain I was looking for, but how about the rainbow?"

I kept on driving. A little while later, the clouds cleared up and the sky was a magnificent blue. Then, there it was - the rainbow I had been looking for.

This was not your regular little rainbow, either. This one was huge, larger than I had ever seen. It seemed wider than any rainbow I'd ever seen, and it seemed to fall right in the middle of the road, but I didn't think that was possible. I kept driving and looking at the wonderful rainbow. It was beautiful; the colors were extremely bright. It still looked as if the foot of the rainbow was falling right on the middle of the road. I kept on driving feeling a little more at ease. It had rained, and I had seen a rainbow; everything was fine.

As I got further down the road the rainbow got bigger and wider. I noticed the cars in front of me were starting to hit their brakes. I could not believe my eyes. The foot of the rainbow was right in the middle of the road and, before I knew it, I was right smack in the middle of it. I hit my brakes hard and almost came to a complete stop. Everybody else was driving at about ten miles an hour and so was I. I was afraid I'd drive right through it and not get to enjoy its overwhelming beauty. I thought it would be as thin as paper and I would pass through it like passing through a curtain.

Wrong! It was huge and thick. It was more beautiful than mere words can describe. The rays of the sun would hit the water and the colors would magnify and explode into more brilliant colors. It looked like glitter floating in the air, except it was transparent and a hundred times brighter and more pure than glitter. Everybody on the road was as amazed as I was. We seemed to be driving through a kaleidoscope. The blues came in all shades. The reds, the yellows, the pinks all were floating and giving off their own individual beams of light and color. It was as if you could reach out and touch them and hold them in your hands. I held my hand out the window and the rays of colors lit up my hand as they gently touched my skin.

This must be the pot of gold that folklore talks about, one of the world's richest beauties. In all its magnificence and brilliance, it was a beauty that could only be experienced to understand; it was beauty in its purest form.

My drive inside the rainbow lasted five or ten minutes, some of the most exhilarating minutes of my life. When I think about it today, I still get a warm feeling. It was my answer. It was my sign, the sign I had received every time I moved, the sign telling me everything would be okay.

I once tore all of the ligaments and shattered the cartilage of my left knee playing volleyball. Rode and some of my other friends got me a little plaque with a rainbow and the inscription, "In order to see the rainbows, we have to endure the storms." How fitting and comforting for me during a time of anguish and pain. Eventually I moved back to Austin and Rode and I married. And yes, it rained on that day, too, but that was fine because the rainbow came out later to tell me everything would be okay.

Thank God for rainbows.

We Have Lift Off

When my wife Rode and I were first dating, I
was always on my best behavior. Like all people
who first start dating, we did all the normalities
that first come with courtship. We talked on the
phone for countless hours. We took long walks.
We held hands everywhere we went. You know -
la-la land type of things. In those early stages
there was nothing she could do or say that both-
ered me and vice versa. Or, at least I'd like to
think so.

As in the early stages of all relationships,
there are things about ourselves that we tend to
hide. Things like, the real you. I was never
crude, rude, or insensitive. I was the perfect
gentleman. I think in her mind I had no flaws,
and I was her knight in shining armor.

As men, when we first start dating someone,
we can be easily convinced to do things that we
wouldn't normally consider fun and entertaining.
Things like the symphony, a ballet, or even an
opera. One day, Rode asked if I would accompa-
ny her to a Valentine's banquet hosted by the
singles club of her church. This entailed a
romantic dinner, some nice music by an invited
singer, a guest speaker talking about "love," and
dressing up in a nice suit - which meant wearing
a tie.

In my mind I was thinking, "What? Are you nuts? I hate wearing suits and ties! I'm not going to some fancy hotel in a monkey suit to eat an overpriced meal, listen to someone sing a bunch of ballads, and listen to some guy talk to me about love!"

Of course what I said was, "A Valentine's banquet! That sounds like lots of fun."

Needless to say, that little white lie led to lots of shopping, endless hours at the mall, and the trying on of what seemed like 1,000 different dresses, and 5,000 pairs of shoes that all looked the same to me. I was in shopping hell and I pretended to enjoy it the whole time.

The big Valentine's banquet finally came. We were dressed to the nines and we looked like a million bucks. I picked her up in my sparkling hand-washed car. When we arrived at the fancy hotel, we strolled into the hotel lobby with style and grace. We ran into some friends of ours and we did the idle chitchat. We walked into the elegant banquet room like we owned the place. My chest was swollen with pride as I pranced around like a peacock.

The chandeliers were set at low to give a romantic feel in the air. There were red heart-shaped balloons everywhere and everybody seemed to be in a floating-on-air type of mood. After endless introductions to most of her friends and all of the visiting, we finally sat down to eat.

The waiters and busboys waited on us hand and foot. Most of the guys looked nervous except for me.

I was calm, cool and collected. I was firing on all cylinders that night. I was funny when I needed to be, and I was honest and sincere the rest of the time. After everything was said and done, and before I knew it, the whole evening was over. The night had been a success of good manners and pleasant conversation, and I was flying high. My sweetheart's eyes were sparkling, and I could tell she knew she was in the presence of a real smooth operator. I had wowed her all night, and there was definitely love in her eyes.

As we were walking back to my car she commented on how much her feet hurt because of the shoes she wore. Being the suave guy I was being that night, I offered to carry her the rest of the way. Of course, at first she refused, but after a lot of assurance by me that it would be O.K., she agreed. The car was only about thirty feet away. After a few giggles and some awkwardness, I stooped over to pick her up. I placed my left hand around her mid-back and the other behind the bend in her legs. With one big swoop, I took a deep breath, and I began to lift.

Then, all of a sudden, without any intention by my part, there was a loud blast from the seat of my pants that seemed to shake the parking garage. In a split second I thought of many excuses: "Did you hear that car with the torn muffler?" Or, since we were near the airport: "Boy those airplanes sure do make a whole bunch of noise when they take off." But, I couldn't say a thing - the red flush in my face said it all. Then, the laughter came. Not only from my new sweetheart and me, but also of the people who just happened to be walking up behind us.

After this shining knight of hers started showing a little rust in the seat of his armor, my sweetheart, being the good sport she is, said, "It's O.K. It's just that I'm a little heavier than you expected with all the food that I ate tonight."

Of course, that didn't help, because she said it as tears of laughter fell from her. I battled through my embarrassment and continued carrying her all the way to my car, all the while laughing and trying to give a witty response for my seepage, to no avail. My image, like my suit of armor, was tarnished.

Through the years we have shared many more embarrassing incidents, but after that night I knew that if she was able to see past my inflatulation with her that she was one of the great ones.

Thanks, Babycakes.

Nothing I Ever Wanted, But More Than I Could Ever Dream Of

———— *2-8-'99* ————

We have all heard the saying, "Thank God for unanswered prayers!" So many times in life, we seem to have an idea that we think would be perfect, and many times we get the total opposite, but it ends up being better than our original plan. The good Lord seems to intervene and sets us straight: what we *need* can be much better than what we want. It's not an easy task, especially for me, to accept what the Almighty has in store for us, because in our minds what we want far outweighs anything else.

I remember when I was a child my family went through some financial hardship. We weren't dirt poor, but we were close. When I was eight or nine, I went to Donna's annual Halloween Carnival where Dad was a volunteer worker in the ring-toss booth. There was an assortment of prizes from toy jewelry to clothes, divided into three or four shelves, the bottom for the least expensive and the top for the most. The pegs on the board you tossed the rings to were color coded to match the shelves: ring the blue peg and win anything on the blue shelf. Of course the higher the shelf the fewer the pegs.

On the top shelf I spotted a game of Monopoly. "Man, I sure would like that Monopoly game," I said to myself. I decided to give it a try. I stepped up and gave my quarter to one of the volunteers, not my Dad. After the instructions from the volunteer, I looked at the shelf the Monopoly game was on and it was blue. I needed to ring a blue peg. Unfortunately, there were only a couple of blue pegs.

I took a big swallow and made my toss. The ring seemed to float on air for an impossibly long time. Finally, it hit the blue peg and jumped up and what seemed to be off the peg. Then it landed snug around the peg. I jumped for joy in excitement. I won! I won the Monopoly game I wanted so much. By this time, Dad had seen me win and I saw him begin to shuffle through some of the stuff on the top shelf. I looked at him while asking myself, "What is Dad doing?" He pulled out this set of clothes, pants and a shirt, which seemed to be my size, and signaled me to choose them. I acted as if I hadn't seen him and told the volunteer I wanted the Monopoly game. I was not going to be denied. After getting my game, I quickly turned to make my getaway. I didn't get too far. Dad quickly caught up with me and pulled me to one side and scolded me for not choosing the clothes.

I knew I was wrong in what I had done, and I couldn't look him in the eye. I knew we were on a tight budget; if I had chosen the clothes, that would be one less set of clothes he would have to buy. So he made me go back and exchange the Monopoly game for the clothes. As it turned out though, I was able to wear those clothes for the whole school year, and they were pretty cool looking for something my Dad picked out.

I just couldn't see the big picture back then. Dad was able to save some money, and when you're on a limited income, that's pretty hard to do. The Lord knew what was best for me, and Dad made sure I knew what that was.

When I graduated from college, I wanted to buy a car. I spotted a new Pontiac Fiero I thought would be a dream. I really and truly wanted that car. It was all me. It was sporty, fun, and, well, just plain perfect. Or so I thought.

Well, I went to the Pontiac Dealer with Dad and my older brother P.J., and we talked the best deal we could. I filled out all the paperwork and signed my name on the dotted line and waited for approval. I kept thinking that in a couple of days I'd be cruising in style and the world would be my oyster. As luck would have it, I was turned down for the loan. The problem was that, aside from my new job, I had no prior work experience and no credit history. Banks and other lending institutions weren't willing to take a chance on me.

The salesman tried to talk me into a less expensive new little Honda Accord. I didn't want any part of it. I knew the Fiero was the perfect car for me. The salesman and I talked about a co-signer. "Would that help?" I asked.

He said, "Yes, but you have to understand that you are a young male under the age of twenty-five, and your insurance alone is going to be more than your car payment, because the Fiero is considered a sports car. Besides, the Honda is a much better car than the Pontiac."

Boy, that infuriated me. I thought he was just trying to make a sale. I looked at the Honda and thought, "It certainly doesn't look better."

Finally the salesman said, "Look, if you really want the Pontiac, what you should do is buy the Honda and pay on it for a couple of years. That will give you some credit history under your belt to show the banks, and then you can trade it in for the Pontiac."

Reluctantly, I agreed. I bought the Honda and was pleasantly surprised at its comfort and reliability. The whole time I owned that little car, I kept thinking that it was only temporary. I was, after all, going to trade it in for something better in a couple of years. The thing was, there wasn't anything better that was as affordable and had as much to offer as my little Honda. As it turned out, I kept it for many years and drove more than three hundred thousand miles in it. As for the Fiero, its maladies and reputation for break-

ing down caused Pontiac to discontinue it.
Thank God for not answering my prayers.

As I was growing up I had this picture in my
mind of the perfect woman. The one I would
marry when I was twenty-one or twenty-two, but
not later than twenty-four. She would have a
light complexion, long hair, light brown eyes, not
be shy, and she would have to be Catholic. Being
Catholic was a big deal because we were going to
have a big Catholic wedding with a big reception
and dance afterwards. We would have children
right away so I could still be young and have
plenty of energy to teach my boys to play baseball. After all, that was my favorite sport and it
would be theirs, too. I could actually picture this
in my head.

Most of all, I could picture my wife, and the
day I met her I would know she would be the
one. That is what I wanted, and in my mind,
nothing else would do. I had opportunities to
date girls that didn't quite fit this description,
but it never lasted long because none of them
were the dream girl I had concocted in my head.

So I started praying for her. Then the
Almighty stepped in and delivered Rode into my
life. She came to my apartment to visit my roommate with a group of girls from his church.
There she was - dark complexion, short hair,
dark eyes, shy, and a Southern Baptist. In other
words, the total opposite of the girl I pictured in
my head.

Yet I found myself extremely attracted to Rode. She had just moved to Austin from Raymondville, Texas to attend the University of Texas. Dago, my roommate, used to go to the church in Raymondville where her dad was the preacher. Not only was she a Southern Baptist, but her dad was a Southern Baptist preacher. Absolutely none of the things I was looking for in a woman.

Dago and I did almost everything together, except go to church. We were both big sports nuts. We played a lot of softball, basketball, and volleyball together. One day, Dago invited me to play volleyball with him and some church friends, and, as always, I accepted. There, I got to see Rode again. It had been a few months since the first time I had met her. I still found myself attracted to her, and I couldn't believe it. "What is wrong with me?" I kept asking myself. "She is nothing like the woman you're looking for. Just forget it." It wasn't too hard not to pursue her because I rarely saw her, at least not until summer rolled around.

Once summer arrived, we played more and more volleyball. We went to tournaments that lasted all day. We practiced just about every day. So I started seeing Rode more and more. I couldn't fight it anymore. Just before she went back to school, I sent her a dozen roses and a song I wrote for her professing my love. Rode was speechless. I can still remember getting her phone call at work after she received the flowers and song. She thanked me a million times. She kept saying how sweet I was and that she didn't know what to say. Lucky for me she felt the same way about me as I did about her.

We have been married five and a half years after dating five years before that. Rode totally changed my life and the way I see things. I cannot put into words what I feel for her and what she has been in my life. My life has definitely been blessed during the decade I have dated and been married to Rode. She has been there, beside me, ever so strong for me, to lean on when times seemed bleak and rough.

Rode has a look in her eye that I have never seen in any other woman in my life - a look of total devotion and love even when I think I am not worthy of such things. It's not one thing in particular that she does, but a culmination of all the little things that make her ever so special to me. Even though I am far from perfect, she has a way of making me feel I am. Even though I am not all that great to look at, she makes me feel like all men pale by comparison. It's the way she looks into my eyes, the way she holds my hand, the taste of her lips when she kisses me, the way she laughs at my nuttiness as if I were the funniest person alive. It's the way she is always ready to say, "I'm sorry," even though she may not be at fault; and the way she easily accepts my apology when I'm the one who's wrong. It's the way she smiles at me when I walk into a room, like a child receiving a treat she has wanted a long time. It's the way she holds me and soothes me and lets me know its all going to be okay when everything seems hopeless. It's the way she makes sure she says, "I love you," several times each and every day. But most of all, it's the genuine love I see in her eyes when she looks at me, or holds me close, that make me feel like the luckiest man on earth. She is my strength and the air I need to breathe, and without her I would definitely be less of a man.

A brother at my hometown church once said, "A woman is not meant to walk behind you like a pet to be treated like a dog, nor is she meant to walk in front of you as a vision to be treated like an idol. She is meant to stand and walk beside you as your partner and your equal."

I'm glad Rode is my partner, but there is no way I could ever be her equal. Rode, with her dark complexion, short hair, dark eyes, shy, and Southern Baptist. Nothing I ever wanted, but more than I could ever dream of. Thank you, Lord, for not answering my prayers; most of all, thank you for my wonderful and beautiful wife Rode.

I love you, Babycakes.

God's Little Gifts

11-15-'00

I have many recollections of the blessings
the good Lord has bestowed my family in the
past years. Some small and some big, all wel-
comed with a smile and open arms. Some were
momentary, some lasted a little longer, and some
have lasted to this day and God willing, they will
be with us for the rest of our lives. The blessings
have come in different shapes and forms, but
nonetheless, all have left a lasting impression in
my life.

When I was twenty years old, I was living
and working in Houston and far away from my
family. My family lived in Donna, a small south
Texas town about six or seven hours drive, and
even though I tried to visit as often as I could, it
was never often enough. I would get homesick on
my way back to Houston and all I longed for was
my next trip. Eventually I adjusted, and though I
wish to this day that I could live closer to my
family, the blessing I received in return for that
desire was that I was able to do a little growing
up. Even though it was a little sooner than I had
hoped for, my life changed, and I was no longer
my family's baby boy.

For twenty years, though, I got to enjoy the
reign of "el coyote," - spanish nickname for
youngest child. Mom would always introduce me
as the baby of the family, and it was nice to be

101

treated differently because I was the youngest. I was spoiled and a little brat most of the time; however, if you ask my siblings, they will say I was a spoiled brat *all* of the time. Even though I was, they were always there to guide me, protect me, and comfort me. It's hard for me to imagine what my life would be without them, and I thank God for the blessing they have been and remain in my life.

When I was twenty years old, my whole life changed with a new home, new friends, and new roommates. But of all the things that changed my life when I was twenty, none of them changed my life more than that little miracle that was sent down from heaven to our family on November 19, 1985. That was the day my niece Debra Lynn, the most beautiful baby girl I had ever seen in my life, was born to my sister Betty and her husband Ernie. From the moment she was born, I knew she was special. Not just because she's my niece and family, but there has always been something about her that has made her stand out. She was the one who took my place as the baby of the family. The first time that I saw her, she was wrinkly and precious like all babies are, but the moment she made eye contact with me and gave me a quick smile, I knew she was a gift from God and that she would be a blessing to our family.

From the beginning, Debra was always sharp as a tack. She was so smart and talented that it always amazed me how someone so young, small, and fragile could grasp life so effortlessly. As the years have passed, I have seen Debra grow from a baby to a young lady, and the only thing that has been able to keep up with her intelligence is her beauty, two things she has been blessed with abundantly. I have so many fond memories of Debra that if I put them down on paper, I would still be writing when kingdom comes.

Debra came to bless our family in a time that we needed it most. Our family was going through some very challenging times as we tried to deal with growing pains and financial and emotional distress. Unknowingly and innocently, she helped hold our family together. She personally made me forget our misfortunes and allowed me to concentrate on the good things. She helped me realize just how precious life really is. She brought life, togetherness and focus into a family that was heading in all different directions.

There was the time she was outside Mom's house squeezing some hot peppers. After a while, the acid of the peppers got to her and started burning. Unfortunately, without knowing, and before it was too late, she rubbed it on her face and arms. I can still see her running into Mom's house with a look of anguish in her face and her mouth wide open trying to scream and not being able to. She turned in every direction and finally, out came this loud scream along with a whole bunch of tears. It took us a while to figure out what had happened because we couldn't get her to calm down enough to tell us what was happening. Finally we were able to calm her down by icing her down, but it took a long while.

Then there was the time she took it upon herself to give herself a haircut. She had long beautiful black hair. She must have been tired of it, because one day at Dad's office, she hid behind the reception desk and proceeded to cut her own hair. I could tell my sister Betty wanted so much to get mad at her, but she looked so funny with her crooked and lopsided hair, that we couldn't help but laugh, so she only got a little scolding.

Then there was the time my brother Eli came home with a pair of tennis shoes that lighted up with every step. Her eyes exploded with excitement when she saw them. Eli was trying to explain to her that he was going to give them to her, but for some reason he wanted her to wait until her mother got there so that she could see them and tell him Debra's size. Debra couldn't wait; the more Eli tried to explain, the more she wanted them. Eli didn't have a chance. Debra came up with a million excuses for why she should put them on right away, until he either got tired of arguing with her, or he finally gave up because he knew he was fighting a loosing battle. If there is one thing that she has always been able to do, it is argue her point. If she ever decides to be an attorney, I pity anybody who goes up against her.

Then there were the times I would tease
her about being the baby of the family. I would
tell her, "For twenty years I was the baby of
the family!"

She would always respond, "Well I'm the
baby of the family now."

We would go back and forth with that for a
little while until one of us got tired; of course, it
was usually me because, as I said, she would
argue her point to the death.

Then there were her ballet and dance
recitals. I still remember her first one. There
were fifteen or twenty little ballerinas in little
pink tutus running and jumping on stage. Debra
looked so beautiful in her little outfit, and you
could see her excitement while she was perform-
ing. I'll always remember the look in her mom
and dad's eyes when she was out there dancing.
I could see they were nervous for her, but most
of all I could see the genuine love and pride they
felt for their little girl. Their pride in her rubbed
off on all of us as we all shared in the joy and
celebration of the baby of the family.

Whether it was her birthdays, her recitals,
or her antics, somehow Debra captivated us all,
and we were able to put off the world for a little
while and enjoy being a family.

Now, as I see the beautiful young lady
Debra has become, I hope she realizes just how

special she is, not only to her mom and dad, but to all of our family and me personally. And as she goes through the growing pains of adolescence, I also hope she realizes just how much she is loved by us all. Although it may seem as if we may not quite understand her, and all of what it takes to be a teenager in today's world, I hope she knows that we will always be there to support, pray, comfort, and care for her.

There are many things I will always associate with change in my life. Rain and rainbows is one. Debra is another. She came into my life, and I was able to pass the torch of the "baby of the family" to her, and she made it shine like a beacon in the night that transforms darkness into day. In a sense, I will always associate her with my transformation from babyhood into adulthood. As I look back at all the blessings that God has bestowed upon me, I realize that sometimes the best blessings are the blessings that come in little packages like Debra, God's little blessing.

I love you, Debra.

Parenthood

3-18-'02

When I was growing up in my father's house I had many ideas about what it would be like to have my own children. I was going to be the ideal father. I was going to play with them tirelessly through the night and take them to the park and to baseball games. I was going to teach them to play baseball, how to ride a bike, how to shoot their first BB gun, and mostly, just be their best friend.

My hometown barber in Donna, Joe Flores, has told me on many occasions that one does not know what it is to be a son until one is a father. By the same token, one does not know what it is to be a father, until one is a grandfather; very prophetic and very true. When Joe first told me that, I thought I knew what he was saying, but it wasn't until my own children were born that I really understood the wisdom of his words.

Last night, my youngest son, Benny (1 yr. 9 mos. old) fell off his brother Johnny's bed. He was supposed to be in his little car bed that is safe and low to the ground. Instead, like many nights before, he climbed into Johnny's bed from his little bed and fell asleep. I was on our home PC playing games, and my wife Rode was in the kids' play room, when about 11:40 p.m., we heard a big thump followed by a loud wail. Rode and I rushed into the kids' room and there was Benny on the floor, next to Johnny's bed, crying in what seemed to be excruciating pain. Rode picked up Benny and noticed a bunch of blood coming out of his mouth and a big bruise and knot on the upper right part of his forehead. The blood came from biting his lip during his fall. Rode cuddled Benny to try to pacify him. I went to the kitchen and wet a small towel with warm water to try to clean the blood out of his mouth. I also got an ice pack from our freezer to place over the knot on his forehead. He definitely didn't like the ice pack and began to wail even louder. Rode was able to calm him down after a long while. "How could we have let this happen?" we asked ourselves.

Thoughts raced through our heads as we tried to come up with new room scenarios to prevent this from happening again. We decided Benny would sleep in our room just for one night. I got the mattress from his little bed and put it on the floor next to our bed. I told Rode we needed to figure something out by tomorrow evening so Benny wouldn't try this again.

Just two Fridays prior, Benny had been on the seat of a small plastic picnic table at day care when he fell off and broke his right collarbone. Now this. Benny is so small, fragile, and innocent. How could I have let it happen? I was supposed to protect him from all of these mishaps. "I have to try to do better." I told myself.

Sophie (4 yrs. 10 mos. old) is our middle child, Daddy's little girl, and Rode's equivalent to an Austin Powers Mini-Me. Sophie continually stubs her toes and scrapes her knees. She usually has a bruise somewhere because she is always running into things. Just the other day she and Johnny were running around inside the house and as she turned the corner to go to her room, she stubbed her pinkie toe into the corner of the wall. She fell to her knees and immediately started to cry in obvious pain. I ran to her side and picked her up, rubbed her little foot, and let her know it was okay to cry and reassured her that she hadn't broken her little toe. A month ago, we went to visit our family in south Texas. Sophie and Johnny were eating breakfast in my mother's kitchen, and Sophie was swiveling back and fourth on her stool. I told her to stop so she wouldn't fall on the tiled floor and hurt herself. She stopped for a little while, but then I saw her pushing the swivel stool she was sitting in back on its hind two legs and letting herself fall back down on its four legs and laughing. Again, I told her to stop because she was going to get hurt. I turned away to get her a napkin, and when I looked back at her, she had pushed her swivel stool back on its hind legs again. However this time, the swivel stool's hind legs slipped on the tiled floor, sending her straight back. It all looked like it was happening in slow motion as I tried to reach and catch her before she fell, but I wasn't fast enough. She fell to the floor on her back with her little feet in the air. I picked her up and cradled her to try to comfort her. She was so surprised and in so much pain that her mouth was agape and tears were gushing out of her little eyes, but she wasn't making any sound. Finally, out came a terrible cry. After a long while, I was able to console her. If only I had been more stern with her, she wouldn't have fallen. If I were only quicker and more attentive, I would have been able to catch her and she wouldn't have been in so much pain. Sophie is so small, fragile, and innocent. How could I have let it happen? I was supposed to protect her from all of these mishaps. "I have to try to do better." I told myself.

When my oldest son Johnny was born on February 13, 1995, he was born with what is medically called a hemangioma. It is better known as a strawberry birthmark. The hemangioma was on the bridge of his nose between both eyes, more towards the right eye than the left. It really wasn't all that noticeable when he was first born. It just looked like a little red spot, like a rash, about half the size of a dime. In the ensuing months it grew dramatically, so much that it started to block his vision in his right eye. By the time Johnny was six months old, it had grown to about an inch and a half in diameter and protruded about an inch out. The whole front surface of the hemangioma was red, which is why it's referred to as a strawberry birthmark. The reason that it's red and protrudes is because there are a whole bunch of blood vessels clustered together, pushing at the surface of the skin. Some hemangiomas are small and some are huge. Johnny's was not considered huge or small. Hemangiomas are actually not all that uncommon, and some doctors consider them hereditary. They will eventually disappear after eight to twelve years if left alone. However, they do possess a dangerous side: it is very difficult to stop them from bleeding if they are ever poked, cut or lacerated.

Johnny's doctor recommended we take Johnny to a pediatric plastic surgeon to get an opinion on whether Johnny would need an operation. He was concerned that if we didn't have the hemangioma removed early enough, Johnny would develop lazy eye or some other vision problem due to the blocking of his right eye. For more than two years we took Johnny to several different doctors who wouldn't treat him, but recommended us to other doctors and specialists. It wasn't until my friend Ed Rios told me to go see his dad that we were actually able to get something done. Ed's dad was one of the first plastic surgeons in the Rio Grande Valley, a four-county area in the southernmost tip of Texas. It was just before Thanksgiving '97 when Ed came by my office and told me he was going home for the holidays. He asked if I had some pictures of Johnny he could show his dad. I did, and Ed took them. On Thanksgiving morning we got a phone call from Dr. Luis Rios. He asked us a bunch of questions about Johnny and what the doctors had done to help him. I explained my frustrations with all the runarounds the doctors and specialists were giving us. I told him the only treatment that anyone had suggested was to inject Johnny's hemangioma with steroids to see if that would stop its growth.

Dr. Rios told me not to let anyone do that. He asked if any of the doctors or specialists had done a CAT scan on Johnny. I told him, no. He asked if they had at least taken any x-rays. Again, no. Dr. Rios was shocked. He couldn't understand why doctors would want to inject Johnny with steroids without even knowing what was underneath the hemangioma. He told us, sometimes when hemangiomas are in the area that Johnny's was, the nasal cavity is not completely closed and the brain sack could be exposed. He said if that were the case, injecting him with steroids could prove fatal.

I was in complete shock and utterly disgusted. The whole situation infuriated me, and I was determined to straighten it out. Dr. Rios then gave us some good news and lots of hope. He told us that Dr. Kenneth Salyer, a cranio facial specialist friend of his, practiced in Dallas. Dr. Rios said that Dr. Salyer was one of the best specialists in the country for cases just like Johnny's. Dr. Rios even made an appointment for Johnny to see Dr. Salyer. The only problem we had was that our medical coverage was an HMO. Dr. Salyer was in Dallas, and we lived in Austin. HMOs usually don't allow (or pay for) you to visit to a doctor who is out of your HMO's network area. At that point, I really didn't care - if the insurance wasn't going to pay, so be it.

Johnny's health was more important to us than anything in the world.

The following Monday morning, after the Thanksgiving holidays, I called my insurance company and learned, as suspected, they did not want to cover Johnny's visit to Dr. Salyer. I argued with the customer service representative and pleaded my case. I explained what Dr. Rios had explained to me and that the situation was life-threatening to Johnny, my only son, our first borne. She wouldn't budge. I asked to speak to her supervisor. She gave me her name and put me on hold for nearly fifty minutes. I guess she thought I would give up, but she guessed wrong.

Her supervisor finally came on the line, and I expressed my frustration about what had been going on – or, not going on - with my son for the last couple of years. I explained that the doctors and specialists in Austin who were under their HMO umbrella were giving us the run-around. I told her what Dr. Rios had explained to me and how this could be a life-threatening situation. I argued with her for what seemed an eternity. She told me that she did not have the authority to grant what I wanted. I asked to speak to her supervisor or, better yet, the person who actually had the authority to grant my request. She gave me her name and put me on hold again. After waiting another thirty minutes, her supervisor came on the line.

Again, I pleaded my case. By this time my frustration level was almost through the roof - like a teapot's high pitched whistle when the water reaches boiling it's point. I seemed to be fighting a loosing battle. I explained again in detail what Dr. Rios had told me and that this could be life-threatening. I asked for her name and direct number and she gave them to me. At the end of my rope, I told her that if she didn't grant my request and something happened to Johnny due to this hemangioma, I was going to come after the insurance company, and I would call her personally to let her know my son had died because she refused to grant him the treatment he deserved. I told her I hoped that she was going to be able to live with that decision.

She paused for a while, cleared her throat, then said, "I am going to call our regional manager in charge of the Texas region and explain to her what you just explained to me, and she will call you back here shortly." Then her whole tone changed. She no longer sounded inconvenienced, but rather more understanding. She assured me that everything would be okay.

Sure enough, about thirty minutes after we hung up, the regional manager called me. She apologized for all the red tape and asked me to explain to her in my own words what had happened. I told her my frustration about what had been going on with the doctors and specialists who were under that HMO's umbrella. Instead of trying to find a viable solution to Johnny's ailment, they just kept shuffling us off to other doctors. Over the previous two years we had seen just about every specialist on their list and each refused to treat Johnny. She kept apologizing while I was detailing our ordeal. I explained to her who Dr. Rios was and what he had told me. After going over every detail, she said she was going to take care of everything. She told me she would call me back in just a few minutes with some information and apologized again for our treatment.

Not too long after we hung up, she called back. She told me that Johnny's doctor's office would call to set up an appointment to see Johnny and to give us a referral to see Dr. Salyer in Dallas. I thanked her for her time and cooperation, and she apologized again and reassured me that all was going to be okay. Sure enough, as soon as I hung up the phone with her, my phone rang. It was the doctor's office, calling to set up an appointment for Johnny for the following morning.

When Johnny, Rode, and I arrived at the doctor's office the next morning, the receptionist asked who we were. I told her and she said to hold on for just a second. Instead of the usual forty-five minute wait in the lobby, we were taken straight back to one of the patient rooms. Again, instead of the usual thirty-minute wait for the nurse and then the doctor, the doctor came in as soon as we got to the room. She looked at

Johnny briefly and said, "So you need a referral for Johnny to see a specialist in Dallas?"

"Yes we do," I replied.

"No problem," she said. She asked for the name of the doctor Johnny was going to see and gave us the referral right then and there.

We were finally able to see Dr. Salyer and he recommended surgery. By the time Johnny went through the operation he was already three years old. Everything went better than expected with the procedure; however, when he first came out of surgery, his whole little face was swollen. I remember my heart dropping when I first saw him that way. It puffed up to the point that both his eyes swelled shut the first night at the hospital. His face was bruised from the surgery (sort of like Sylvester Stallone in Rocky), and he looked like he was in tremendous pain. Couple that with not being able to see because his eyes were swollen shut and you can imagine what a traumatic experience it must have been for Johnny. He cried for his mama. He cried for his daddy. Every time he cried, Rode and I reassured him we were there. We stayed with him in his hospital room all day and night. After a couple of days in the hospital, we brought Johnny home. Little by little the swelling went down and the scar from the surgery healed, but I'll never forget the expression on his little face when they finally wheeled him away to do the surgery. He had that look of innocence. I can still see his little face all swollen after his surgery. Even now it aches my heart. Johnny is so small, fragile, and innocent. How could I have let it happen? I was supposed to protect him from all of these mishaps. "I have to try to do better." I told myself.

There is a deep pain that hurts to the center of your soul when bad things happen to your children or they get hurt. It's a pain that can't be described, but it makes you ache all over. Its like a piece of you dies every time something bad happens to them. Every ounce in your body yearns to somehow switch places with them so you can absorb their hurt and their pain. Mom once told me that there is a saying in Spanish that says, "Si tu esposo o esposa muere, te llaman biudo o biuda. Si tus papases mueren, te llaman huerfano. Pero, si se te muere un hijo o hija, no hay nombre que se da porque no hay palabra que compare con el dolor" Which translates to, "If your spouse dies, you are called a widow or a widower. If your parents die, you are called an orphan. However, if one of your children dies, the hurt is so deep that there is no name that is given, because there is no word that compares to the depths of the pain."

I cannot begin to imagine the hurt and pain I would feel if something happened to any of my children. I thought I knew what love was when I was growing up, but now I know that I was mistaken. That isn't to say the love I have for my parents, brothers, and sisters isn't real love. It's that it fails by comparison when you measure it to the love that parents have for their children.

As a child, I thought my parents were too strict, not in tune, without a clue at times, and even antiquated in their ways. As a father, I know the truth. And as I struggle with the trials of parenthood, I now know why my parents were the way they were. My parents were actually very much in tune, very wise, and actually very much ahead of their time.

However, I still think they were a little strict.

Thanks, Mom and Dad.

Go Daddy, Go!

11-5-'97

I was coming home from church the other day and as I was getting on the freeway my son Johnny yelled, "Go Daddy, Go!" Immediately a big smile came to my face. Unknowingly, my son had triggered a childhood memory of growing up in my father's house.

When I was growing up, my parents would take us just about everywhere with them. Whether it was to visit my grandparents or to the park or to the grocery store, we would all pile into the station wagon and take off. Being the youngest, I usually rode in the very back seat that faced backwards. The gunner position. My brothers and I were always fighting for position and space. "You're on my side," one of us would yell.

"Stop touching me," the other would yell back.

I can remember my brother Manny, famous for drawing imaginary boundary lines, would take his hand and run it up and down the seat as if he were cutting it with a knife while saying, "This is my side and that is yours. Stay on your side." Of course that just meant while he wasn't looking you would touch his side and giggle about it; but if you got caught it meant a shove and an, "Haste pa ya!" which loosely translates to, "Scoot over there!" Typical brotherly love.

We were always playing games and everything seemed like a competition to me. I hated to lose. I was the biggest crybaby when it came to losing. Whether it was a simple game of marbles, or football, or baseball, it didn't matter - I hated losing. We couldn't finish playing until I won, or else I would throw a temper tantrum. At least that is what my brothers and sisters tell me.

I tend to see it a little different. One of the games I always played in my head on our trips in the family station wagon was car racing. I'd pretend we were in a race and every car Dad passed was a victory. Of course, every car that passed us was a loss. I would build all this excitement in my head and get caught up in the race. Nobody else knew about my game. It was all in my head. Dad was a good driver and he won most of the races, but when he lost, it would kill me. I would be totally caught up in the excitement in my head, and all of a sudden, there was a car that came out of nowhere to pass us. I couldn't stand it. It was like a phobia of some sort. It was pure fear.

The fear of losing, I guess. Losing, the thing I hated most in the world then. My emotions would get the best of me and I would yell to Dad, "No te dejes, Daddy!" which translates to "Don't let him beat you, Daddy!" My heart would beat a hundred miles an hour and, if Dad didn't speed up, I would tell him again, but with more emotion, "Please, Daddy! No te dejes." It didn't take much pleading to get Dad to stomp on the gas though. He would lay that hammer down on that big Plymouth station wagon and we would pass them right back again, giving me the much needed win for my ego and, best of all, vengence on the guy that beat us earlier.

Sometimes though, Dad would not speed up and it would break my heart. I would begin to cry out of anger and frustration that Dad would allow someone else to beat him. That was incomprehensible to me. Why would he want to lose? No one wants to lose. I would throw a temper tantrum as a last resort to get my way. I would be screaming and yelling, "Come on, Dad, you can do it. Please! Don't let them beat us." That worked most of the time. Dad would speed up and give chase to the mangy mongrel that passed us earlier. Slowly my tears would stop and I would start looking for the car that overtook us. As soon as I would get it in my sights, I'd grin with happiness and excitement and start yelling, "Go Daddy, Go!"

The closer Dad got to the enemy, the faster the adrenaline would flow through my blood. In most cases Dad wouldn't let me down. Zoom - we would speed right by them and victory was mine again. There wasn't anything I liked more than being faster than everybody else on the road.

My obsession with winning all the time slowly diminished as I got older. For Dad though, it was too late: I turned him into a lead foot. He continued to drive like a bat out of Hell, even though I was no longer begging him to do so.

Later when I started driving, I redeveloped this obsession with not letting anybody pass me. If someone passed me, I would step on the gas and pass them right back. I was willing to go as fast as the car that I was driving could go to not let someone pass me. Of course, that didn't go very well with the police officers that frequently pulled me over. Don't ask me how, but luckily I was able to talk my way out of most of those encounters with the law. Even though it is not as strong a feeling as it used to be, I still don't like the idea of somebody passing me.

Who knows? I may never get over it, because every so often (more often than not), I get the urge to be in front of the pack again. Going faster than everybody else.

They say that life seems to repeat itself and that children are just mirror images of their parents. In this case it certainly seems true. My son Johnny has a lot of the same characteristics and mannerisms as I do, and I can see myself in the things he says and does. Sometimes I can sit there and just look at him for hours in amazement and see the things that he sees, for his eyes were mine once. And on that night coming home from church, I could definitely hear myself yelling at my dad through his voice when he yelled out to me, "Go Daddy, Go!"

I love you, Johnny.

In Dreams

───────── *6-24-'02* ─────────

One of the things I loved when I was growing up in my father's house was visiting my
grandparents - Mom's parent's - in Mexico. They
lived just south of the Rio Grande on a huge
farm that had a long drive lined by trees and ole-
anders on each side. When my Grandfather (or
Abuelito, Spanish for grandfather, as I always
called him) would see us coming down the long
drive, he would chase down two chickens and
wring their necks for supper that evening. His
dogs would greet us at the entrance to his drive-
way and escort us to the main house.

Farmland as far as the eyes could see sur-
rounded the main house, barn, stables, and cor-
rals, and I always felt at peace when we were
there. I can remember playing in the cornfields
and chasing the chickens for fun. We sometimes
went fishing on a big canal that ran close by.

Grandma (or Abuelita, as I always called
her) would take some fresh hot corn tortillas and
sprinkle some pure cane sugar on them and roll
them real tight for me. The heat from the tortilla
seemed to caramelize the sugar and it tasted just
like candy to me. *I can still taste them now.* I
spent my time eating good food and having fun
during our visits. Nighttime would come and I
can still see the sun set behind a silhouette of
palm trees that lined a far-off dirt road. It never

failed, as we would all start piling back into Dad's station wagon, Abuelito would always give me some money for the road.

He knew that most of the time on the way back home, Dad would stop in Las Flores, a little Mexican border town that had the nearest international bridge back to Texas, to buy some groceries that were cheaper in Mexico. He would always tell me to buy whatever I wanted and as much as I could with the money he'd given me. Mom would never want me to take the money, but somehow Abuelito always managed to sneak me some.

Abuelito, Abuelita, and I always shared a special relationship. My brothers and sisters would always tease me that I was Abuelita's favorite grandson. The reason they told me, was that when I was young, I looked just like my Tio (Uncle) Misael (or Chael, as they called him). When I was three or four years old, Tio Chael died from internal bleeding due to a farming accident when he was in his early twenties. Abuelita commented frequently about how much I looked like Tio Chael and that always made me feel special. Even though I can't really remember much about him, because I was so young when he died, I do have vague recollections. I'm pretty sure it was him we went to see just before he died. All I remember was entering a room where a very sick man lay in bed. He reached over and said something to me as he ruffled my hair. However, I can't remember what he said, and every time I replay it in my mind I can see his lips moving, but I can't hear what he's saying. I also remember attending his funeral shortly after that. I can still hear Abuelita crying over the gravesite. I guess to Abuelita I was Tio Chael reborn, and maybe that's why she treated me a little more special than my brothers and sisters.

Abuelito and Abuelita moved to Texas from Mexico in May of 1975, because Abuelito started getting very sick and needed medical attention. Mom and her brothers and sisters decided to have Abuelito see a doctor in Texas, because of the better health care here in the U.S. The doctors found that Abuelito had some blockage and hemorrhaging in the back of his brain caused by a blow to the head. While in the hospital, Abuelito lost all consciousness and the doctors did not give him much of a chance. They told Mom that, even with surgery, his chances of survival were very slim. I can remember seeing Mom's face filled with grief. The night of the surgery we prayed and prayed for what seemed like eternity. After five or six hours of surgery the doctors came out and told Mom, my uncles and aunts that it was all in the hands of the Lord. If he could survive the next twenty-four hours he just might make it. I'm thoroughly convinced a miracle took place that night, and that the good Lord saved my Abuelito's life, because by morning the doctors were all shocked by his improvement.

After Abuelito came out of the hospital, our relationship continued to get better. Abuelito and Abuelita were now living in a retirement community in Mercedes, Texas, about ten or twelve miles from Donna, and I was able to see them more often. We would visit them at least once or twice a week and Abuelita always had plenty of delicious food. I would sit and listen in awe to Abuelito tell me stories of his childhood and life on the farm, and Abuelita always made sure that I had plenty to eat and that my cup was always full of coffee. It wasn't just the stories and the good food, it was the bond that we shared that made everything special.

As the years passed and I grew older, things remained about the same for us. I'd still visit them once or twice a week and Abuelita still had plenty of delicious food to eat. Abuelito's stories, although somewhat repetitious, were still fascinating. One thing Abuelito could always do, is make me laugh. He had a terrific sense of humor. I remember this one time it was pretty cold (for south Texas), and we were having a party over at our house. I told him, "It's very cold outside, Abuelito."

Without batting an eye he turned to me and said, "Heck, I usually go out dressed in nothing but underwear during weather like this." Or he would joke with Abuelita whenever pretty girls would walk by. He'd tell Abuelita, "If they ask, you tell them you're my sister."

Unfortunately, Abuelito passed away on March 5, 1991. Abuelita survived him another nine years. However, equally as unfortunate she suffered from Alzheimer's for most of those years. Their deaths hit me very hard and to this day it makes me very sad. When Abuelita died, I don't want to say it was a relief, but after seeing what Alzheimer's had done to her, she no longer seemed to be the Abuelita I knew and loved. It was almost unbearable to see her that way. I still remember the last time I saw her and that she actually recognized me. I walked into Mom and Dad's house, and she was sitting in the living room. As I came up to her she smiled at me and her eyes lit up the room. She stood up and said, "Johnny, it's so good to see you. How have you been?" as she gave me a big hug. In that hug, which probably only lasted a few seconds, I was able to feel the lifetime of love she'd had for me. It was a feeling of warmth and serenity that told me all would be okay. My sister Betty and my brother Eli teased me that I must have been some sort of angel, because she hadn't recognized anybody else that morning. We sort of chuckled about it for a bit, but in the back of my mind it was also very comforting that she actually remembered who I was. In the same sense though, it also made me sad because of what Alzheimer's had done to such a wonderful lady.

Through the years I've often mentioned to myself, and sometimes in a loud whisper, just how much I miss them. Sometimes, when I'm feeling down on myself or going through something tumultuous, I'll say, "I sure wish I could talk to you Abuelito. I could really use one of your stories right now." I know that sounds a little crazy, but it usually makes me feel a little better.

A little more than a year ago, I was struggling with a personal conflict and I couldn't decide what I was going to do. I remember having a hard time going to sleep one night because I couldn't stop thinking about my predicament. Rode had been sleeping with my son Benny in his room because he was having trouble sleeping with a fever. Shortly after I finally fell asleep, I started dreaming. It was all crazy, like most dreams are. In my dream I walked into Abuelito and Abuelita's house in Mexico. There, lying on a bed was Abuelito, all covered up in a white sheet. It seemed to be his wake. As I started to make my way to the next room, he called out to me much to my surprise, "Hello Johnny." ˙

I responded, "Abuelito? I don't understand, you're supposed to be dead. Everybody is sad and crying because they think you're dead."

"Who is in the next room there?" he asked.

"Everybody is. Mom, Tio Pepe, Tio Lupito, Tia Mari, Tia Nena, Tia Vila, and Abuelita." Aside from Abuelita, I had mentioned all his children.

He asked, "Pepe is here, too?"

"Yes." I said.

"That's good, because he's always making everybody laugh. What is everybody doing?"

"They're all sad and crying because they think you're dead." I said.

"Well, tell them not to worry and that I'm okay."

I went into the next room all excited and said, "Hey everybody, don't cry, Abuelito is okay! He's up and awake!" But it was as if no one could hear me. Everyone just continued to cry and mourn. The more I tried to convince them he was okay, the more they seemed to cry. I couldn't believe it. I couldn't even get one of them to get up and come and see that he was fine.

Abuelito then said to me, "Come on, let's go for a walk." So we ended up leaving everybody there in their house. As we started walking down the road, he turned to me and asked how I was.

I told him I was fine, but lately I had been struggling with some personal issues.

He turned to me and said, "You need to start living your dreams of today before they become your regrets of tomorrow."

"What?" I asked.

He repeated, "You need to start living your dreams of today before they become your regrets of tomorrow."

I was speechless.

He then said to me, "Don't go around trying to please everybody all the time. Do what is in your heart and you will always be happy."

It sure sounded simple enough.

"But what if I follow my dreams and fall on my face, or end up disappointing my family?" I asked.

He responded, "At least you'll know that you tried. What would be terrible is if you never tried and wound up wondering, 'What if I had done this or that?' Or worse, 'I should have done this or that.' So stop worrying about things that are beyond your control and start taking control of the things you do have control over."

"I'm not sure I understand."

So he said, "You're worried about 'what ifs' instead of asking yourself, 'Why not?' and adjusting to anything else. Things happen all the time that force us to make changes in our lives. Change is not something to fear. Its what we make of it that matters."

As we traveled throughout our journey during this dream, Abuelito kept on encouraging me. We walked for what only seemed a little while, but we covered many miles. He said not to worry - God was always going to be there to help me through any obstacle in my path.

We caught a ride with a friend who was in a rush to get to California because his boss needed him there A.S.A.P. We drove with him through the beautiful Hill Country of central Texas and convinced him we needed to stop at a quaint hilltop country store with a café. I noticed my friend was all tense and the pressure of him getting to California was killing him. Abuelito started giving him the same advice that he had just given to me. I noticed that he was giving the same excuses that I was, but by now none of his arguments made sense to me.

I jumped in and tried to explain what Abuelito was trying to tell him. I then started to feel all the anxiety and tension being lifted from my body. It was as if I went through some sort of transformation. The more I explained Abuelito's advice, the more I believed and accepted it. It was amazing. All of a sudden things were becoming very clear to me and my predicament was no longer a matter of conflict anymore; and I knew what I needed to do.

As my friend drove away, leaving us behind at the country store, I turned to Abuelito and said, "I think I'm starting to understand now."

We started walking again, and he continued to reassure me and advise me. The one thing he kept going back to and that has stuck with me to this day is, "Start living your dreams of today before they become your regrets of tomorrow."

I was beside myself and I couldn't believe all that was happening. It all seemed real. The strange thing is that, I remember knowing he was dead in my dream, but that didn't matter. He made me laugh and he awed me with his conversation, and for that brief moment, it felt like I had traveled back in time to my childhood. *"God, I miss him and Abuelita!"*

Somehow, time always seemed to stand still when I was with them, and in my dream it was no different. Before I knew it, we were walking in the front door of my house in Austin. I didn't want the dream to end, so I tried to keep the conversation going. I asked him if he understood me when I prayed in English, because he only spoke Spanish while he was alive. He said that there was no language barrier in Heaven, so it didn't matter in what language I spoke, he would still understand. I tried to get as much information from him as I could, and I remember thinking to myself, "I hope I can remember all of this when I wake up."

I even asked him who was going to win the next Super Bowl, but he refused to answer. I pleaded with him to tell me, but I couldn't budge him. It felt as if he were reading my mind, because he said he couldn't tell me because he didn't want me betting on the game. Even though I promised him that I wouldn't, he still refused. The only clue he said to me was, "It's going to be a team that you least expect to win." I'm glad he didn't tell me, because in the back or my mind, I was hoping to bet on the game.

We finally made it back to my bedroom. He reassured me that all was going to be okay and that he was fine. He reminded me one last time, "Start living your dreams of today before they become your regrets of tomorrow."

And I smiled at him as if to say, "I know, I know." I got into bed and he pulled the covers up to my shoulders.

I said, "I love you Abuelito."

He leaned over and kissed me on the forehead and said, "I know, I love you too."

At that moment, I awoke, and I swear I felt his kiss and his presence.

I then smiled and said, "Thank you, Abuelito."

I couldn't go back to sleep. I was full of energy and elation and I couldn't wait to tell Rode. The whole thing was uplifting, and I finally felt at peace with myself. I went to work the very next day and wrote on the marker board in my office, "Start living your dreams of today before they become your regrets of tomorrow." Many of my co-workers came by and asked where I had heard that phrase, and every time a big smile would come to my face as I said to them, "I got that saying from my grandfather."

Ever since that dream, I've felt certain serenity in my life. I try to listen more to what my heart has to say, and not what I think the world wants of me. I try not to let small things worry or get to me like I used to. And things beyond my control, I try to leave them in the hands of my Lord for it is only He who has real control. As for my dreams of today, this book just happens to be one of many dreams I hope I can live through to fruition. And the only regret would have been to pass this off as only a dream.

Did it really happen? Was Abuelito really there? And just how true were his words that night of my dream? I'm not sure I have the answer you may be looking for, but I will tell you this: the New England Patriots won the Super Bowl that year, when nobody on God's green earth gave them a chance. Even though the thought did cross my mind, I didn't bet on the game. Like I said, I don't have any answers, but I would like to leave you with some advice a very wise man once passed on to me.

"Start living your dreams of today before they become your regrets of tomorrow."

Thanks, Abuelito.

Special Thanks to:

Howard Wolfson who not only helped me publish this book, but was also the one who finally convinced me to do so.
And to all my friends who read and proof read my stories and kept encouraging me to follow my dream,
Laura Steiert, Karen Jordahl, Carrie Mora, David Flathmann, Becky Arredondo, Raul Hoxie, Jill Ryon, Jorge Bermudez, Tonya Browning and Mike Morrison.
And to David Schlosser, who helped us with the final editing and creative input.
And to all my friends at TxDOT